THE
LOW-INCOME
CONSUMER

To Lawrence Feinberg,
whose quest to satisfy curiosity
about all things guided and inspired

THE
LOW-INCOME
CONSUMER
Adjusting the
Balance of Exchange

Linda F. Alwitt
Thomas D. Donley

SAGE Publications
International Educational and Professional Publisher
Thousand Oaks London New Delhi

For information address:

 SAGE Publications, Inc.
2455 Teller Road
Thousand Oaks, California 91320
E-mail: order@sagepub.com

SAGE Publications Ltd.
6 Bonhill Street
London EC2A 4PU
United Kingdom

SAGE Publications India Pvt. Ltd.
M-32 Market
Greater Kailash I
New Delhi 110 048 India

Printed in the United States of America

Library of Congress Cataloging-in-Publication Data

Alwitt, Linda F.
    The low-income consumer: Adjusting the balance of exchange / by
Linda F. Alwitt, Thomas D. Donley.
        p.   cm.
    Includes bibliographical references and index.
    ISBN 0-8039-7211-3 (cloth: acid-free paper).—ISBN 0-8039-7212-1 (pbk.:
acid-free paper)
    1. Low-income consumers—United States.   2. Marketing—United
States.   3. Poor—United States—Finance, Personal.   I. Donley,
Thomas D.   II. Title.
HC110.C6A65   1996
658.8'348—dc20   95-41731

This book is printed on acid-free paper.

96   97   98   99   10   9   8   7   6   5   4   3   2   1

Sage Production Editor: Tricia K. Bennett
Sage Typesetter: Andrea D. Swanson

Contents

Acknowledgments

We thank the Kellstadt Center for Marketing Analysis and Planning of DePaul University for financial support for some of the effort that went into writing this book. We are especially appreciative to Robert Pitts, Director of the Kellstadt Center, for his continuous encouragement and support for studying marketing issues related to the poor consumer.

Many people helped us in this project, and we apologize to those we may have inadvertently not mentioned. We thank Alp Arditti, Daniella Iannicelli, Sally Mlodock, Chang Shu, and Niti Vaish for help in compiling references. Susanne Cannon championed and taught us how to use geodemographic mapping. We thank Robert Alwitt, Suzanne O'Curry, Robert Pitts, Jerome Williams, and several anonymous reviewers for their comments on drafts of some of the chapters. Fr. Paul Golden, Fr. Jay Jung, Sr. Donna Ryan, and Sr. Susan Sanders of DePaul University were most supportive of this project. Conversations with marketing colleagues at meetings of the Association for Consumer Research as well as Public Policy

and Marketing, at DePaul University and Queens University, and with
Connie Evans of the Women's Self-Employment Project were very helpful
in pointing out topics to discuss and clarify. Mary Ann Gordon, Cindy
Clark, and Patricia Clickener always offered encouragement when needed.
We thank our editor at Sage, Marquita Flemming, who was most enthu-
siastic about the project and helpful at creating the context for generating
new ideas and tonalities.

Finally, we very much thank our spouses, Bob Alwitt and Terry Donley,
for discussing issues frequently and at length, for pointing out relevant
newspaper articles, and most important for being patient and understanding during the course of this project and others.

Linda F. Alwitt
Thomas D. Donley

1

Introduction

> When asked what she would wish for if she had a magic wand, Ebony took about a minute to answer. "A house," she finally says. Then silence. "Food," she adds. Then pauses. "A stove." "A table."
>
> —Hopfensberger (1992, p. 1a)[1]

Affluent consumers worry about size, style, color, and flavor when they shop. Poor consumers worry about just obtaining the basic necessities—"For *which* child should I buy shoes?" Yet, lack of purchasing power is but one of many challenges faced by poor consumers when they go out to buy goods and services. A single mom may have to pay for a car pool to do her weekly shopping at a supermarket that offers goods at a fair price. A man who can only find part-time work may pay extremely high fees when he cashes a check. In other words, problems faced by poor consumers differ from those faced by more affluent consumers.

In this book, we describe some obstacles faced by poor consumers. Poor consumers not only face difficulties in obtaining basic needs such as food and housing, they also face obstacles in financial transactions such as paying bills and obtaining cash. They often pay more for the same goods more affluent people buy and are offered shop-worn or outdated merchandise—at the same price everyone else pays or more.

> Credit cards are banned from the house; she is still ashamed of how they ran up a huge debt and had to declare bankruptcy. The creditors were so aggressive they came and demanded her engagement ring and Virgil's wedding band. (A description of a working wife who earns $1,000 a month in Gibbs, 1995, p. 19)[2]

The poor do not have the safety nets taken for granted by the more affluent: insurance, accumulated savings, social security, or pensions. Because of these and other problems, poor consumers also face higher levels of stress. They are more prone to address the stresses of everyday life by television watching and cigarette smoking. We describe these obstacles one at a time, but we must remember that poor consumers face these problems simultaneously.

Who are poor consumers? They generally have less education and work experience and are less likely to have grown up in two-parent families. They are typically younger than the rest of the population. Clearly, poor consumers are disadvantaged by more than simply a low level of income. Some of their demographic and other characteristics influence their consumer decisions—what they buy, where they buy it, and how they are influenced to buy one rather than another product category or brand.

> You know, Mrs. Clark, it sure wasn't very easy for me to talk our credit manager into taking you on. Yessir, he's a tough old bird. But I got you those beds and that fancy washer-dryer. Ever see anything so nice? Now don't you let me down on those payments after I went out on a limb for you, hear? (Greenberg, 1980, p. 383)

The goal of marketing is to provide for the needs of consumers at a profit to the business and by an increase in shareholder wealth. The means to making a profit are not always in the best interests of consumers, and the poor do not wield sufficient power to safeguard their interests as consumers. As a result, transactions between marketers and poor consumers are often balanced in favor of the marketer. Marketers generally treat poor consumers as they do all consumers and apply the same marketing tactics. When marketers do think of poor consumers as a group with different needs, they may face an ethical conflict. The heart of the conflict is often a clash between marketers' personal obligations to themselves or their firms versus their obligations to the society that provides the infrastructure in which the business operates.

Even if a business considers low-income households as just another group of consumers, in doing business with poor consumers they are confronted with issues different from those they find when they deal with more affluent consumers. This is true for both the local distributor on the front line and for the brand manufacturer. For example, on the local level poor consumers may not have the money to purchase needed products outright at the time of purchase. Businesses frequently are not willing to make the necessary credit arrangements, however, because of the perceived high risks in dealing with low-income consumers. Businesses justify their decisions on the basis of their past experiences. Due to the popular perception of the business risks of the poor marketplace, many businesses have fled poor neighborhoods, making an already dire situation even worse for poor consumers.

Poor consumers are frequently just as distrustful. Poor consumers often see merchants who continue to operate in poor communities as outsiders bleeding the community of scarce resources and offering little value in return. Listen to a complaint about intercity buses by a woman delayed in her travels on intercity buses between Chicago and Louisiana:

"They are making money, and they don't care if they inconvenience you. They know rich whites are flying, so only blacks, foreigners and poor whites are catching the bus" (Thomas, 1995, p. 3).[3]

Brand manufacturers or marketers not on the "front line" of distribution to poor consumers also face conflicts. Although they strive to meet consumer needs at a profit, due to market pressures they may decide that the most profitable route is simply to ignore the poor consumers who spend less on goods and services than more affluent consumers. When marketers do consider poor consumers as a viable market segment, the goods they market may be of low quality or have a negative effect on the consumers themselves or on society. Notice how much advertising for tobacco and alcohol products is plastered across billboards in poor neighborhoods.

In general, the immensely greater resources of businesses ensure that in transactions with poor consumers the poor are often at a disadvantage. In this book, we describe the imbalance of marketing exchanges between marketers and poor consumers and offer suggestions for ways to put the exchange on a more even keel.

A number of questions can be raised about poor consumers and their relationships with marketers. Here are some of them:

- Why do poor people spend more than their cash incomes?
- In estimating market potential, why should businesses rely on more than just marketing research reports?
- Why is the public stereotype of the poor person misleading?
- Do more affluent people really know what poor people consume, or do they just assume the poor throw money away on chips, candy, and liquor?
- Why do the poor have more hassles in handling their financial affairs than more affluent people?
- Why do the poor have to spend proportionately more on food and housing?
- How can poor people help themselves be wiser and more efficient consumers?

The answers to these questions have implications for many institutions in our society. Businesses can find profitable opportunities in the poor marketplace. Public policymakers can be alerted to injustices that can only be solved by regulation. Social service agencies can focus on areas that need educational intervention and help poor people initiate actions to better their lives as consumers.

THE CONTEXT FOR BUSINESS
ATTITUDES ABOUT THE POOR

Attitudes of marketers about poor consumers are molded by our society. They exist within the context of a society's attitudes and practices about its poorer members. Daniel Levine (1988), in a historical analysis of welfare in four nations, noted, "The most powerful influence on the shape of each version of the welfare state was the history, institutions, and perceptions within that country" (p. 283). Attitudes about poverty and welfare and how they influence marketing to poor consumers are founded on several different perceptions about the United States. These perceptions are shared by businesspeople, marketers, and other affluent members of U.S. society.

What are these perceptions? First, the United States is perceived to be a land of abundance. Immigrants still arrive in the United States expecting to see the streets paved with gold. Economic indicators on an aggregate level support this perception (e.g., Cateora, 1990, p. 321). The United States is perceived as a land of opportunity where self-sufficiency is highly valued. The implication of these beliefs is that hard work is all that is required to become financially self-sufficient. The Great Depression of the

1930s was a watershed in that it called this implication into question. In part because of the dissonance of the Great Depression with previous attitudes about the incidence of poverty in the United States, the number of innovative social welfare programs in the United States was increased in the 1930s.[4] To this day, however, Americans draw comfort from the belief that the poor are somehow less deserving and are in their present straits due to personal faults or prior poor decisions.

Individualism has been identified as a powerful value in the United States from early days (Bellah, Madsen, Sullivan, Swidler, & Tipton, 1985; Tocqueville, 1839-1840/1945). The strong belief in the value of individualism implies that Americans have an obligation to provide for themselves and not rely on the state or other institutions for support. In a nation where each citizen presumably has equal opportunity to obtain economic resources, those who fail are perceived as only having themselves to blame. Individualism, together with the U.S. heritage of Puritanism, is a basis for the strong work ethic in this nation. Americans believe that able-bodied people have an obligation to work and that work leads to success. It is our strong work ethic that encourages negative attitudes toward the poor (Mead, 1992).

Second, we tend to offer support to those who are similar to ourselves. This is a nation founded in ethnic diversity, accepting of geographic mobility, and primarily urban. Most of us live more among strangers than among friends or acquaintances. Yet, we seem to yearn for a sense of community. Wanting to help "our own" explains this nation's reliance on church-based charity to provide for the poor until the middle of the 19th century (Higgins, 1981). The heterogeneity of the population discourages public support for centralized aid as the poor are easily perceived as "different" and not part of the "community."

Contributing further to these social mores are negative attitudes to government intervention to address poverty problems. Because this nation was founded as a federation of states, the role of a centralized government has always been carefully monitored and controlled. The issue of states' rights is one reason why we have consistently tended to place the burden of providing for the poor at a more local level. This heritage argues against centralized programs to cope with poverty. It also encourages a demand for a minimal role of government. Another barrier to governmental interventions for the poor earlier in our history is that prior to the 1930s strong trade unions opposed social welfare by the state because it diminished the power of the unions over their members (Higgins, 1981). In the past, government has tended to be considered the provider of last resort rather than the provider of first resort. The federalist nature of the U.S. government still holds considerable appeal and with the Republican Congress of 1995 stands to be the guiding force of welfare policy for the foreseeable future.

As a result of influences such as these, social benefits in the United States have been more acceptable to the public if they apply to everyone, such as social security, than if they are specific to one group, such as Aid to Families With Dependent Children (AFDC). Social benefit to a segment of the population, such as welfare, has traditionally been acceptable only when provided to "deserving" poor. Although the definition of deserving shifts over time, it historically includes only those persons physically incapacitated or unable to care for themselves due to age or death of a provider. The able bodied have not historically been included.

In summary, public attitudes about poverty in the United States tend to be harsh. A 1990 Harris survey reports that 46% of the sample strongly favor requiring people to work to receive welfare, and 60% agree that welfare discourages young women who get pregnant from marrying the father of the child. Programs for the *deserving* poor receive support, however—only about a quarter of the population is in favor of abolishing welfare programs such as job training (24%) or food stamps (29%) (Harris Poll, 1991).

Nonetheless, substantial government aid is budgeted for the less fortunate in the United States. In 1994, spending on welfare cash assistance programs amounted to approximately $46 billion (Schiller, 1995).[5] In addition, costs of in-kind welfare programs (i.e., food stamps, Medicaid, housing assistance, and school lunch programs) were estimated at another $173 billion in 1992. Other social insurance programs such as social security, Medicare, unemployment insurance, workers' compensation, and veterans' benefits amounted to an additional $552 billion in 1993. These are clearly substantial sums and have attracted the ire of antiwelfare advocates across the political spectrum in the United States.

WELFARE IN THE UNITED STATES AND OTHER NATIONS

Are attitudes about poverty and welfare in the United States different from attitudes in other parts of the industrialized world? Let's put attitudes about poverty in the United States in perspective by considering poverty and welfare in a context that extends beyond the United States. Consider how poverty levels and practices about the poor in the United States compare to those in other developed nations.

The U.S. welfare system has been criticized as mean spirited by a number of authors, and the United States has been characterized as being a "welfare laggard" among the developed nations (Higgins, 1981). Despite the seemingly large amounts of government expenditures, there is some truth to these allegations. Historically speaking, welfare programs in the United States emerged gradually, starting with workmen's compensation prior to World War I and continuing with old age pensions and unemployment insurance in 1935 and some forms of national health insurance in the 1960s. In contrast, state welfare programs in Germany and in Denmark were adopted in the late 19th century (Levine, 1988).

Not only has the United States only recently joined the welfare states, but it also allocates a smaller percentage of government expenditures to antipoverty programs. In terms of the percentage of government expenditures on social security and welfare, the United States ranks 20th of 96 nations, with 28.4% of total expenditures used for this purpose. Nations that spend a larger proportion for welfare include Switzerland, Sweden, Denmark, the Netherlands, Norway, Finland, Canada, Italy, and the United Kingdom (Kurian, 1991). Another criterion for comparison, net taxes (gross taxes minus transfer payments to the population), also places the United States low on the list. The United States has a low rate of net taxes compared with other developed nations, 18.7% of the gross domestic product. In a comparison of eight developed nations, only Japan has a lower rate, at 16.8% of the gross domestic product (Sandmo, 1991).

In terms of welfare benefits, the United States is the only one of the 10 developed nations in the Luxembourg Income Study without a child allowance as part of the social policy system. It also has the lowest level of benefits for poor families with children (Smeeding, 1991). In addition, the United States tolerates a higher level of income inequality than do other developed nations. Compared to 10 other industrialized nations, the United States has the highest percentage of its population with incomes less than one half the median income level (Blackburn, 1994). Finally, the United States ranks first in the percentage of poor families with children and second only to the United Kingdom in the percentage of elderly poor (Smeeding, 1991).

In summary, although the United States devotes substantial sums of money to its less fortunate citizens, the spending is low relative to other developed nations. Furthermore, political winds are blowing to reduce government aid to the poor. This is consistent with societal mores that revere self-reliance and a perception of abundant opportunity for those willing to take advantage of it. It is in this context that marketers and poor consumers meet in the marketplace.

WHAT THIS BOOK IS ABOUT

Our goals in this book are threefold. First, we identify the poor. We describe the characteristics of the poverty population in some detail in order to be able to understand the array of problems faced by poor people in their roles as consumers. Second, we describe conflicts faced by poor consumers when they enter the marketplace. These problems illustrate how marketing exchanges between poor consumers and businesses are often balanced in favor of business and worsen the welfare of low-income consumers. Third, we suggest approaches to bring the marketing exchange between poor consumers and businesses into better balance.

It is important to bring the marketing exchange into better balance for the sake of society as well as poor consumers. An imbalanced marketing exchange isolates poor consumers and contributes to alienating them from the rest of society. There need not be losers when a marketing exchange is put in balance. This is because the total quantity of what is exchanged by all parties is not necessarily constant. In other words, marketing exchange need not be a zero-sum game. An important implication of this assertion is that when poor consumers and society get more from an exchange, marketers need not necessarily get less. Consequently, balancing a marketing exchange benefits not only poor consumers and society but also marketers. Marketing exchange with poor consumers is discussed in more detail in Chapters 2 and 9.

These issues are of keen concern to marketers, economists, social service workers, and public policymakers involved with poverty in the United States. Poor communities offer marketers a way to expand their businesses. Because many markets are difficult to expand today in the most profitable segments of affluent consumers, other sources of profit must be found. Some businesses have sought to increase profits by entering international arenas. There is another option—targeting less affluent Americans. Economists often consider other aspects of poverty, but they have paid little attention to the behavior of poor consumers and consumption patterns of the poor. The issues discussed here begin to fill that void. For social service workers and public policymakers, we offer ways to help poor consumers address some of their problems.

The three chapters that follow provide background about marketing and about the poor needed to understand problems of poor consumers. We introduce three key marketing concepts, define poverty, and outline the poverty population in the United States. The marketing concepts presented in Chapter 2 lay the groundwork for discussing ways in which exchanges between marketers and poor consumers can be put into better balance. In Chapter 3, we discuss how poverty is and can be defined, as well as sources of financial resources for poor people. In Chapter 4, we describe the poor in the United States in terms of their demographic and some of their behavioral characteristics.

The next section of the book covers some specific problems poor people face as consumers. In Chapter 5, we discuss problems related to the basic necessities of life—food, housing, and transportation. We also discuss consumption of "sin" products by poor consumers. Chapter 6 covers how the poor manage their finances and their uses of money-saving techniques. The focus of Chapter 7 is how poor consumers learn about products from marketers. We describe the media poor consumers favor and products for which they see advertising and other marketing communications. In this chapter, a way is presented to think about how well poor consumers cope with marketing communications such as advertising. Chapter 8 is about price discrimination and the limited accessibility of goods and services for poor consumers. We present evidence of higher prices being charged to people who live in poor neighborhoods and discuss the concepts of price discrimination and price differentiation. We include a case history of the geographical locations of different kinds of retail outlets in one city, Chicago, to illustrate the breadth of the problem of limited retail access for poor consumers.

In the last section of the book, we draw out the implications for more equitably balancing the marketing exchange between poor consumers and businesses. We present a revised model of marketing exchange with poor consumers and draw implications from that model for a more equitable balance of exchange.

NOTES

1. Reprinted with permission of the *Minneapolis Star Tribune*.

2. Reprinted with permission of *Time* magazine.

3. Copyright © 1995 by the Chicago Tribune Company. All rights reserved. Used with permission.

4. These programs included the Federal Emergency Relief Administration (FERA), the Civil Works Administration (CWA), the Works Progress Administration (WPA), and the Social Security Act.

5. Three programs account for this spending: Supplemental Security Income (SSI), Aid to Families With Dependent Children (AFDC), and General Assistance (GA).

2

Some Relevant Marketing Concepts

> They did some [welfare] cuts a couple of years ago, and the business
> dropped big-time. . . . Ninety-five percent of our customers are on
> public aid, and it is their only source of income.
>
> —The co-owner of a food and liquor store
> near a public housing development,
> quoted in Reardon and Thomas (1995, p. 5)[1]

Businesses make certain assumptions about the act of marketing when they sell their products. What are those assumptions and how are they relevant to marketing goods and services to poor consumers? What do businesses see as their duties and obligations and those of their customers? In this chapter, we introduce marketing concepts relevant to issues that concern poor consumers. The first is the very basis for marketing, *marketing exchange*. The second is a widely used marketing concept, *market segmentation*. It can be thought of as the basis for this book, in that poor consumers can be considered a market segment. The third concept concerns the roles of *marketing ethics* in transactions between marketers and poor consumers.

MARKETING EXCHANGE

When a poor consumer gives food stamps to a checkout clerk and receives a bag of groceries, he or she is taking part in a transaction that creates a marketing exchange. When a neighbor baby-sits while a single mother goes shopping for shoes for her 5-year-old, they are taking part in an exchange. When a retired man pays a high fee to cash a social security check at a currency exchange, he is taking part in an exchange. When a salesperson in a lease-to-buy furniture store is especially attentive to a poor consumer who could not afford a down payment to purchase furniture outright, he is offering esteem to the customer in exchange for making a sale that may involve usurious interest rates.

Exchange means that one party gives up some of his or her resources to obtain resources from another party. The resources we generally think of exchanging include money, time, goods, and services. The resources we exchange, however, can also include intangibles such as feelings, status, and information.

Exchange is central to the definition of marketing. Marketing assumes that there is a basis for exchange if one person has something of value to another person and the other person has something the first person deems valuable. For an exchange to occur, both parties must feel they have benefited.

What is exchanged may be not only obvious resources such as money and goods but also less tangible resources that come from the *act* of exchanging. The leased-furniture exchange described at the start of this section is an example. Although the explicit resources exchanged are furniture and weekly payments, the intangible resources derive from the good feelings the customer gets from the salesperson during the transaction. In other words, there are psychological consequences to an act of exchange (Bagozzi, 1979). A person may feel he or she made a good bargain or may simply feel satisfied with what was gained from the exchange or may have enjoyed the act of bargaining with the other party to the exchange. Conversely, a person may dislike the process of negotiating for a price acceptable to all parties or be anxious that the money was not spent as wisely as possible. These intangible resources are often considered when businesses attract poor consumers. Listen to a mother of four who is on welfare: "It's a fight to keep your self-esteem up. . . . You go to your social worker and they treat you like nothing" (Davidson, 1995, p. A14).[2]

How long the parties to an exchange are committed to their relationship partially depends on the outcome of each exchange transaction. For example, the item you bought may be of poor quality and not last as long as you expected, or the salesperson may have been unpleasant to you. Reactions to both the goods or services received in an exchange as well as to the act of exchanging may have consequences that extend over time (Houston, Bassenheimer, & Maskulka, 1992). If both parties were satisfied with the outcome, they are more likely to continue the relationship in the future.

People often have ongoing relationships with products, services, and businesses, as well as with people. They frequent the same grocery store or supermarket; they use the same dentist; they smoke the same brand of cigarettes; and they look for the same salesperson. Thus, exchanges may involve a commitment on the part of some or all parties that extends beyond a single transaction such as a purchase of milk and eggs at a convenience store. This is particularly important to both retailers and manufacturers today because they know it is more cost-effective to keep a customer than to win a new customer. As pointed out in Chapter 4, those who are temporarily in poverty are particularly valuable long-term assets to a business.

Marketing exchanges with poor consumers differ from other marketing exchanges. First, marketing exchange is not just the way people do business. It requires relationships with other people, and relationships lead to community, the key precondition for society (Koehn, 1992). Most important, people who have nothing of value to exchange are isolated from the community and treated like strangers. Poor consumers who are limited in their exchanges are isolated from the rest of society by their economic situation. Thus, marketing exchanges with poor consumers serve as a link for them with the rest of society.

Second, a traditional simple exchange occurs between two parties, most often a buyer and a seller. As Bagozzi (1975) noted, however, social marketing exchanges often include more than two parties. Bagozzi's model of the social marketing exchange applies to social rather than economic relationships. For example, his model might include an exchange between a social worker and a client. A marketing exchange with poor consumers might also include governmental agencies (e.g., AFDC), society in general (e.g., charitable donations), as well as suppliers of goods and services. When we consider marketing exchanges that involve poor consumers, we must keep in mind that there are often more than two parties to the exchange.

In the second section of this book, we describe and discuss numerous barriers to marketing exchanges with poor consumers. Consider two points about these barriers: (a) They isolate poor consumers from participation in society as a whole, and (b) removal of these barriers can involve more than merely the consumer and the immediate vendor. In Chapter 9, we reconsider Bagozzi's (1975) exchange model with poor consumers as one of the parties.

MARKET SEGMENTATION

Few marketers view each and every consumer as a potential customer. Marketers recognize that their brand, product, or service is not equally valued by all consumers. Instead, they take one of two routes. They either present their brand to a selected group of consumers in the same way, or they market the brand differently to different groups of consumers. The selected group of consumers to whom a firm presents its brand is called a market segment. By selecting some but not all consumers as potential customers, a firm focuses on a segment of the market and uses *market segmentation*.

If a firm uses market segmentation by presenting the brand to a selected group of consumers in the same way, everything the marketer can control about the brand is the same for all the selected consumers.

What can marketers control about the brand? They can control the features of the product, its price, where the brand can be bought, and how the advertising presents the brand. When a poor consumer selects a well-known rather than a store brand, he or she is strongly influenced by marketing tactics. Marketing tactics used to create a well-known brand include establishing a reputation for quality, value, or good performance over the brand's lifetime; ensuring that the brand is among the limited set of products available in small neighborhood outlets; encouraging consumers to consider its higher price as an indicator of brand quality; and heavily advertising the brand to make consumers aware of it.

Using this approach to market segmentation, the product itself, its price, how the brand is advertised and promoted, and the way in which it is distributed are the same for all of the selected consumers. Furthermore, everything about the brand is optimally designed to make it appeal to the set of consumers selected as those most likely to purchase it. Consider a brand of disposable diapers. A manufacturer of disposable diapers wants to attract the segment of consumers who have very young children. The brand has a single suggested price, one advertising plan, one plan for distributing coupons to potential customers, and one plan for ensuring that the diapers are given appropriate shelf space in stores that are frequented by parents of young children.

In a second approach, a firm might simultaneously market a brand differently to different selected groups of consumers. One example is ready-to-eat cereals. Large cereal firms market high-fiber cereals to adult consumers and presweetened cereals to families with children. Adult consumers and families with children may consist of different groups of people or different market segments.[3]

In a variation of simultaneously marketing a brand differently to more than one segment of consumers, a single product is presented so that it is perceived differently by different segments of consumers—that is, the same brand is "positioned" differently in the minds of consumers from different market segments. Dewar's scotch whiskey has run a dual advertising campaign for many years. "Dewar's Profiles" advertising presents biographical profiles of young professionals who, of course, drink Dewar's scotch. Presumably, the type of person who is profiled is someone with whom the selected consumers can identify or who can serve as a role model for the selected consumers. At the same time, another Dewar's campaign associates the brand with bucolic scenes of Scotland. It is presumed to be attractive to more traditional and older potential consumers of scotch whiskey.

In both of these segmentation approaches, marketers identify the group of consumers who are most likely to be potential customers and develop a marketing plan to attract them. Poor consumers can be considered a market segment. For some products or services, poor consumers may be considered particularly profitable. For example, R. J. Reynolds attempted to introduce Uptown cigarettes to a target market of African Americans in 1990, only to withdraw the brand after consumer challenges to this use of segmentation (Schiffman, 1990). For another example, poor consumers are a key market segment for Western Union. Because low- income consumers have fewer financial management options than do the more affluent, they often rely on money orders and money transfers offered by firms such as Western Union for their financial transactions.

For other products and services, low-income consumers are shunned as potential consumers. The marketing decision to exclude low-income consumers may be based on the perception that this market segment is

insufficiently profitable or offers too much risk. Such a decision is reasonable for certain expensive products or services, such as luxury cars or
financial investment services. By excluding low-income consumers as a
potential target for other products or services, however, marketers may
fail to meet the needs of this segment of the population and may miss a
marketing opportunity. An example is the dearth of supermarkets in
low-income neighborhoods.

For yet other products or services, income is not the basis on which
potential customers are selected. An example is the market segment for
disposable diapers. Except by marketers of low-price brands, low-income
consumers may not be an appropriate separate market segment.

As goods and services used by poor consumers are discussed in this
book, consider whether marketing strategies are—and whether they *should*
be—directed at poor consumers as a separate market segment.

ETHICS IN MARKETING TO POOR CONSUMERS

> Hey, you don't want to do something stupid like complaining and ruin all
> I've done for you, do you? Why make your credit worse than it already is?
> If you start making trouble and we have to cut you off, then where are you
> going to go? Look's like that living room set is beginning to come
> apart—where are you gonna get a replacement except from me? You don't
> want to spoil all this for yourself, now, do you? (Greenberg, 1980, p. 389)

Any discussion of poverty must involve ethical issues. Many of these
issues concern poor members of society in general rather than in their roles
as consumers. Here, we limit the discussion of ethical issues to the poor
as consumers. Three general areas are discussed: the types of ethical issues
that can arise in relation to poor consumers, how ethics are used in the
processes by which people decide what to do, and ethical criteria for
marketing exchanges.

Marketers, consumers, and societal institutions can be the subjects of
ethical issues in marketing. Situations in which unethical behavior by poor
consumers is at issue include behaviors such as food stamp fraud, returning
clothing worn once to an apparel store for a refund, and "skipping out"
on payments. Some of these unethical actions are carried out by all
consumers regardless of income level and some are specific to poor
consumers. Not all poor consumers engage in unethical behavior. What

makes one but not another poor consumer use an unlisted phone to avoid calls from bill collectors? What makes one but not another poor consumer use food stamps to purchase nonessentials? These are questions about consumers' ethics.

Ethical issues that concern society in general include questions like determining the minimum standard of living that the society is willing to tolerate for its poorest members. This question is discussed in Chapter 3. Another ethical question that concerns society in general is determining the roles of the institutions of a society—what aid should be provided by government, religious bodies, community organizations, business, and individual citizens. An example of a more specific question is whether it is ethical for government to provide resources for a transportation infra-structure that benefits its wealthier members and its larger industries, such as roads and airports, compared to more cost-effective and energy-saving mass transportation systems that might benefit less affluent members of society.

One kind of issue that concerns marketers includes questions like whether it is ethical for marketers to treat different members of society in different ways—that is, is market segmentation ethical? Should poor consumers be treated as a separate segment by marketers? If so, under what conditions? Is it ethical to subsegment poor consumers with differ-ent needs based on their differing life situations? For example, at one time, the minimal requirements to define a person as poor was partly based on whether he or she lived in a rural area (on the premise that rural people could more easily live off the land) and on age (on the premise that old people eat less).

Another kind of ethical issue for marketers concerns the products that are sold and the prices charged for them. Is it ethical for firms to market new products with features that may stimulate the market and result in higher profit to the firm if they do not benefit the end consumer and increase the cost of the product line? Is it more ethical to offer a basic line of products? Currently, price discrimination is legally prohibited at the commercial level under antitrust legislation such as the Robinson-Patman Act. Should price discrimination be practiced at the *retail* level, often to the disadvantage of poor consumers, even though it is legal to do so? Should a business charge higher prices or offer less value for the same price to some consumers merely because those consumers, who are often poor, have limited opportunities to seek alternatives?

Another set of issues concerns marketing communications. To what extent should marketers take into account the vulnerabilities of their intended audiences? Should marketing communications directed at poor consumers use persuasion techniques that are particularly likely to be effective with this group of people? For example, should they use role models highly esteemed by that group of consumers?

These are examples of ethical issues that affect poor consumers. It should be clear that ethics need not be written into law and that the law probably only defines a minimal level for an ethical behavior. Societal institutions, businesses, and consumers are often faced by ethical dilemmas in their decisions about actions to take in the marketplace. Businesses have responsibilities to multiple stakeholders, and it is sometimes difficult to prioritize demands from the stakeholders. An individual marketer must balance demands of career ambitions, short-term goals of a brand manager, long-term goals of the corporation, stockholder interests, and the public good. Most people believe we intuitively solve ethical dilemmas, but there must exist some underlying guidelines for solving these problems.

The underlying guidelines we use have been addressed by moral philosophers and business ethicists. What might the main approaches say about ethical problems that concern poor consumers? Some theorists contend that there are universal rules of behavior that apply to everyone, and some of these theorists have attempted to list such binding rules (e.g., Laczniak & Murphy, 1993, p. 35). For example, one might argue that everyone is obligated not to injure other people. If this rule is used by the manager of a supermarket in a poor neighborhood, he or she might discard outdated meat and dairy products to ensure that the products sold are fresh enough to be healthful.

John Rawls's (1971) approach is similar. He asserts, "Each person is to have an equal right to the most extensive basic liberty compatible with a similar liberty for others," and "social and economic equalities are to be arranged so that they are to the greatest benefit of the most disadvantaged" (Laczniak & Murphy, 1993, p. 36). Because Rawlsian theory focuses on the well-being of the least well-off members of society, the needs of poor consumers would come first rather than as an afterthought for business decisions. The idea of placing the needs of poor consumers ahead of all others does not imply that the needs of other consumers go unmet. Instead, the Rawlsian approach reminds businesses and society of the priority of the needs of the poor and other disadvantaged members of the population.

A similar approach focuses on the assertion that "human beings are of basic importance in society and that their inherent dignity as persons entitles them to make certain fundamental claims about how they should be treated by others in society and by society itself" (Mahoney, 1995, pp. 5-6). In other words, people have basic human rights, which are fundamental and universal.

According to another approach, ethical decisions should produce the greatest good for the greatest number of people. This guideline, which weighs benefits against costs, could be used to the disadvantage of poor consumers. For example, it could be used by a bank to justify closing bank branches in poor areas. Bank officials might claim that because the poor are a minority of the population their needs can be subservient to those of the more affluent majority and it is to the benefit of the majority among the stakeholders of the firm to close bank branches in low-income neighborhoods.

These different approaches to underlying processes that direct moral behavior provide guidelines in theory. It is extremely difficult to determine which of them are used by specific people in specific situations, however. An approach that relates ethics to the basis for marketing, marketing exchange, may be more helpful when we consider the poor consumer.

ETHICAL CRITERIA FOR MARKETING EXCHANGES

Gundlach and Murphy (1993) have identified four ethical criteria for marketing exchanges: *trust* that the parties to an exchange will fulfill their obligations; *equity* of the perceived inputs and outputs by parties to the exchange; *responsibility*, or the obligation of each party to the transaction; and *commitment* to the exchange, which implies a willingness to compromise and to amortize the benefits derived from the exchange over more than a single transaction.

All four of these criteria are imbalanced in exchanges with poor consumers. Marketers do not *trust* poor consumers to have sufficient resources to pay for goods or services, and poor consumers do not trust that they will receive the quality of goods or services for which they exchange their limited funds. This may be part of the reason why in the Los Angeles riots, retail stores owned by people perceived to have offered unfair exchanges with the residents were destroyed whereas other stores were spared (e.g., Boyer & Ford, 1992; Chua, 1994). Sellers do not value what poor consumers offer for exchange, so they sometimes extract other, nonmonetary input to obtain what they perceive to be an *equitable* exchange. For example, poor blood donors are treated less courteously than are more affluent blood donors. This is probably because the staff perceives the motivation for donating blood as voluntary by middle-class donors but self-serving—being paid—for low-income donors. As a result, the staff of blood donation centers demean poor blood donors, demanding passivity and compliance and requiring long periods of waiting as though these donors' time is not valuable (Kretzmann, 1992).

Because poor people are not part of the "real" society, marketers may not feel an obligation to carry out their part of the exchange (*responsibility*). For example, a food stamp user noted that supermarket cashiers replenish their supply of change when they discover he is using food stamps; another customer noted that this was the way they exacted an additional exchange value (Rank, 1994). Finally, marketers to poor consumers do not seem to have a *commitment* to maintaining the poor consumer as a long-term customer. They often act as though they are unaware that most poor people are only temporarily in poverty. As discussed in Chapter 4, it may be cost-effective for marketers to encourage low-income consumers to be brand loyal.

The point of discussing marketing ethics is to indicate that marketers are not villains in their marketing exchanges with poor consumers. Rather, they often must select, and sometimes compromise, among demands that create ethical conflicts. These conflicts must be resolved by compromising between short- and long-term benefits and losses and between direct personal and indirect societal benefits and losses.

SUMMARY AND IMPLICATIONS

Marketing exchange, marketing segmentation, and marketing ethics are central issues to consider when thinking about problems of poor consumers and conflicts faced by marketers to them. In subsequent chapters, we describe and discuss numerous examples of imbalanced exchanges between low-income consumers and marketers of goods and services to them. A revised model of exchange is presented in Chapter 9.

Many problems arise because of inappropriate treatment of poor consumers as a separate market segment. There are various reasons for this use of segmentation. It may result from inaccurate perceptions by marketers of the characteristics and resources of poor consumers. It may result from the way a firm prioritizes its obligations to stakeholders, resulting in a higher priority on profit making than social responsibility. It may result from simply not thinking about the poor and allowing situational influences to drive marketing actions—"business as usual."

The popular press reports various unethical actions by the poor, by marketers to the poor, and by other societal institutions, many of which are referred to in later chapters. But ethics involving exchanges with poor consumers have not been systematically addressed by the academic marketing community, with the exception of the marketing of tobacco and alcohol products to the poor (e.g., Smith & Quelch, 1993).

We argue in the following chapters that in marketing exchanges the balance usually does not favor the poor consumer. Poor consumers have some needs that are not being adequately addressed by purveyors of goods and services although their market potential may be underestimated by businesses. We describe instances of unbalanced exchanges and suggest approaches to redressing the imbalance.

NOTES

1. Copyright © 1995 by the Chicago Tribune Company. All rights reserved. Used with permission.

2. Reprinted by permission of the *Wall Street Journal*. Copyright © 1995 by the Dow Jones & Company, Inc. All rights reserved worldwide.

3. Products may also be bought by the same group of people but consumed by different persons in the household—or by the same persons on different occasions.

3

The Definition of Poverty

Unlike some other calculations, those relating to poverty have no intrinsic value of their own. They exist only in order to help us make them disappear from the scene.

—Orshansky (1968, p. 28)

As Mollie Orshansky (1968), the person most responsible for the current definition of poverty employed in the United States, makes clear, the definition and measurement of poverty often is used as a panacea for poverty rather than just a first step toward a solution to the problems of the poor. To discuss the obstacles faced by poor consumers, we must understand the definition of poverty. This chapter is devoted to a better understanding of the poor. It provides background to issues involved when the poor enter the marketplace. If we are to be concerned with problems of the poor consumer, we must know who these consumers are.

Marketing professionals are accustomed to thinking of the poor in simple terms of low income. For example, a marketer to poor consumers is likely to examine their consumer behavior by referring to the annual reports of market survey firms such as Simmons Market Research Bureau, Inc. (SMRB) or Mediamark Research, Inc. (MRI). These reports provide data on usage of products, services, and media for consumers at different income levels. Such data are likely to paint a misleading picture of poor consumers because income alone does not reflect levels of need. What the marketer may actually wish to identify is the market segment that faces severe resource constraints and is more (or less) prone to purchase a particular product. Attempts to identify resource-constrained market segments that focus solely on income and ignore relative levels of need do not capture differences in discretionary income. For example, if the poor are simply defined as families with reported annual incomes of less than $15,000, there will be considerable variation in their consumption patterns. A young single consumer with this income may have much room for discretionary expenditures, whereas a family of four with the same income level would have little. Although low income is obviously related to being poor, formal definitions of poverty also take relative levels of need into account.

Although there is no perfect way to define poverty, discussion of the differential impacts of marketing on poor consumers requires a clear definition of what is meant by poor. Given the consumer focus of this book, we examine poverty in terms of economic well-being rather than in a broader welfare or psychological sense. More comprehensive or alternative poverty definitions may well have merit, but this approach recognizes that we are focusing on the members of society with limited resources to purchase goods and services.

The first step in a formal definition of poverty is to establish a *needs standard,* or poverty threshold. Such a standard implies there is a minimum level of resources that society believes an individual or family should have at their disposal. Three approaches are commonly taken in establishing these standards, or thresholds. The first approach is characterized as *absolute* in that an objective standard is set based on empirically determined needs. The second approach is commonly characterized as *relative* in that needs are set in relation to the level of resources commonly available within the community. The third approach is *subjective* and is based on individual perceptions of requirements. These three approaches typically lead to different poverty thresholds, levels of poverty, and poverty populations. In the first section of this chapter, we outline each of the separate approaches.

Once a set of poverty thresholds has been designed, the resources a household has available to meet the standard must be identified. Aside from cash income, needs standards may be met by in-kind transfers, gifts, insurance payments, and assets. The second section of this chapter is focused on sources of purchasing power available to poor consumers in addition to annual incomes. Given the consumer's ability to borrow and save, some discussion is also devoted to the choice of the appropriate income accounting period. In the appendix to this chapter, we describe the official U.S. poverty thresholds and put them in a historical perspective.

SETTING A NEEDS STANDARD

Poverty thresholds are designed to quantify a level of economic need. They typically distinguish between differing levels of need by taking family size into account. Because income serves as a reasonable proxy for purchasing power, most thresholds are based on income. Poverty thresholds can be classified as either *objective* or *subjective*—objective in the sense that rules can be applied to determine poverty status and subjective in the sense that poverty is defined by a feeling of economic deprivation. This taxonomy of poverty thresholds can be extended to identify two general subcategories of objective poverty measures, *absolute* and *relative*.

ABSOLUTE THRESHOLDS

Absolute poverty thresholds are objective standards focused on estimates of actual needs and the resources necessary to meet those needs. Arbitrary low-income cutoffs frequently used by marketers, although without controlling for need levels, are examples of absolute thresholds. This approach is similar to early government attempts to define the poor. In 1964, the president's Council of Economic Advisors (CEA) proposed categorizing any family of two or more members with annual pretax income of less than $3,000 and individuals with annual pretax income less than $1,500 as living in poverty (Council of Economic Advisors, 1964).[1] The most obvious shortcoming of such approaches is that they are inequitable; the CEA standards proposed in 1964 classified a family of two with $2,900 in annual income as poor and a family of eight with an annual income of $3,100 as not poor.

Consequently, efforts were made to control for differences in family composition to better capture relative economic requirements. Orshansky, at the Social Security Administration, developed a "basic needs" approach to establishing absolute poverty thresholds in the 1960s. This type of needs standard is typically based on the choice of a food basket minimally nutritionally sufficient for a family or individual. The price of this food basket is estimated for different family sizes, and income is added to cover additional expenditures on other necessary items such as housing and clothes. Based on previous research, Orshansky assumed that families spent approximately one third of their income on food and set the poverty thresholds accordingly. This resulted in a set of poverty thresholds equal to three times the amount of income required to purchase a subsistence amount of food—differentiated by family size (see the appendix to this chapter for more details).

Absolute poverty thresholds are appealing because they seem to be empirically based. They roughly estimate what families actually require to function in society, consistent with a minimum decent standard of living. Their greatest strength is allowing easy assessment of changes in the levels of economic hardship in society over time based on a fixed level of needs. Nonetheless, such thresholds and the resulting poverty definitions have serious shortcomings.

The first shortcoming of absolute poverty thresholds concerns how to determine the amount of resources needed for a minimum standard of living. The typical starting point is a set of nutritional requirements. When the Orshansky thresholds were developed, the U.S. Department of Agriculture (USDA) reported four separate estimates of dietary requirements: liberal, moderate, low-cost, and economy. Although Orshansky chose a seemingly reasonable mix of low-cost and economy food plans, Fisher (1992) noted that "families spending for food at the dollar cost level of the economy food plan had about 1 chance in 2 of getting a fair or better diet, but only 1 chance in 10 of getting a good diet" (p. 4). As we shall see in Chapter 5, there is evidence of poor nutrition among poor families.

In addition, even if nutritional requirements are scientifically determined and socially acceptable, the percentage of income that should be allocated to meet them must be determined in order to set poverty thresholds. Orshansky used a multiplier of three based on a review of previous research on consumption patterns of families. But as Watts (1967) noted, this multiplier assumes that other components of the minimum standard follow the same scale economies as food, a proposition that has little theoretical or empirical support. For example, Renwick and Bergmann (1993) accounted for families' differing needs for child care, transportation, and housing costs. Although their approach yields lower thresholds for some poor family types, it yields higher ones for others; their basic needs budget doubles the poverty thresholds for a single-parent family in which the parent works, has two preschool children, and lives in a central city in the Midwest. Some researchers have noted that the poor spend more than one third of their income on food, implying a smaller multiplier and therefore lower set of poverty thresholds; others contend that, over time, average expenditures on food have fallen to as low as 20%—implying a larger multiplier. In summary, estimates of subsistence levels of income are based on assumptions that may not be acceptable to all stakeholders.

Absolute poverty thresholds are argued to be superior to alternatives because they are based on a fixed level of need, but another shortcoming of the approach arises because consumption baskets are anything but fixed over time. As Ruggles (1990) noted, "Constructing a market basket of normal consumption goods 50 years ago, for example, would not have included a telephone, a television, or air-conditioning, but all might be included in 1990" (p. 17). Differences of opinion over what constitutes a minimum set of commodities feed the debate over how poor the poverty population truly is. Robert Rector (1992), a policy analyst for welfare and family issues at the Heritage Foundation, argues that only a tiny fraction of those officially defined as poor meet what the general public considers poverty criteria. As evidence, he notes that in 1989 40% of all households defined as poor own their own homes, raising the question of whether or not the general public considers lack of home ownership a defining characteristic of poverty. This is a problem of identifying the resources counted toward meeting the poverty thresholds rather than a problem of the level of the poverty thresholds themselves, an issue that is explored in more detail in the second section of this chapter.

In brief, absolute poverty thresholds are attractive because of their empirical basis, because they present a fixed target over time and because they are consistent with the concept of a minimum decent standard of living. The faults of such standards are no less real. It is difficult to establish an objective minimum standard, and a fixed consumption bundle will miss changes in consumption patterns over time. These problems can render the thresholds obsolete. Nonetheless, official poverty calculations in the United States are based on absolute poverty thresholds.

RELATIVE THRESHOLDS

An alternative approach to establishing poverty thresholds is based on relative economic deprivation. Families or individuals are considered poor if they do not have the income necessary to meet contemporary standards of living within a society. Those with a substantially lower income than the balance of the population are defined as poor. There is considerable appeal to such an approach, and a majority of European countries have adopted relative definitions of poverty.

One advantage of relative poverty thresholds over absolute thresholds is that they allow for changes in consumption patterns over time. Relative thresholds automatically adjust to prevailing standards of living within a society. As society progresses and the commodities required for participation are upgraded, the definition of poor changes accordingly. In addition, there is little debate over what constitutes a necessary minimum, as the focus is on relative economic deprivation—people are considered poor if they are unable to afford what is considered customary in their society.

Yet, this approach begs the question of what exactly constitutes poverty. How much income guarantees the ability to afford the lifestyle customary in the country? One answer to this question is to set thresholds equal to the income cutoff for the poorest 20% of the population. But to do so clearly imposes the condition that 20% of the population will always be poor, regardless of their income level.

As a result, most analysts propose setting relative poverty thresholds as a percentage of median income. For example, Fuchs (1967) and Rainwater (1974) argue for a threshold equal to one half of median income. The benefits of this approach are clear. As incomes grow, so do the poverty thresholds, guaranteeing a constant relative measure of economic deprivation. It is also possible to decrease the poverty rate by increasing the income of the poorest members of society relative to the balance of the population. A relative poverty threshold, set as a percentage of median income, still retains its distributional aspect, yet levels of poverty can be influenced by economic and political events.

Although setting poverty thresholds at one half of median income may seem reasonable, there is no theoretical justification for this standard as opposed to, say, one third of the median. There is little theoretical guidance regarding the appropriate level of the thresholds relative to the overall distribution of income. Furthermore, the choice of an income benchmark poses difficulties. Although a family's relative position in a society's total population matters, it seems more appropriate to measure its position relative to families of the same size and composition. This presents a problem that can be demonstrated using the distribution of income in the

United States. Family income in the United States increases with family size up to four members and then begins to fall.[2] Poverty thresholds set as a percentage of median family income would decrease as family size increases beyond four members. Economies of scale would be expected to arise as family size increases, but there is no reason to believe that the amount of money required to meet a subsistence level of expenditures would actually decrease as family size increases.[3] As a measure of economic need, relative poverty thresholds clearly leave something to be desired for the United States.

Not only would relative poverty thresholds punish large families in the United States, but they also would not control for actual levels of need. For example, if the threshold is set equal to one half of the median income and family size is not considered, the relative poverty threshold, using constant 1990 dollars, would have been $8,823 in 1950 and $18,421 in 1990. In the 40 years since 1950, a family living at the edge of poverty could have doubled its purchasing power yet still have been categorized as living in poverty (Council of Economic Advisors, 1984, 1993). In a growing economy, a relative poverty threshold could lead to an increase in the number of poor even as the living standards of the poorest members of society rise dramatically. This captures the most commonly cited shortcoming of relative poverty thresholds: They do not allow for an accurate assessment of society's progress against the economic hardships faced by its poorest members. Relative poverty thresholds are better as a measure of the distribution of income than as a measure of economic deprivation. They tell us very little about the level of discretionary income available within a household and how it has changed over time.

SUBJECTIVE THRESHOLDS

The third type of poverty threshold is based on a subjective assessment of what society deems a minimum necessary income. The idea here is that the best approach to determining a socially acceptable level of minimum resources is to survey the members of a society. This is sometimes referred to as the Leyden approach and the resulting poverty thresholds as the Leyden Poverty Lines.[4] The Leyden approach is based on subjective assessments of welfare or well-being and their relationship to the level of income.

A benefit of the subjective approach is that it bridges the absolute and relative poverty thresholds by asking people to assess their actual needs and welfare, which are presumed to increase as society's standards increase. In fact, Hagenaars and Van Praag (1985) estimated that a 1% increase in median income will lead to an approximate one half of 1% increase in subjective poverty thresholds themselves. Because absolute thresholds are unaffected by increases in real median income and relative measures change on an equal percentage basis, subjective thresholds fall at about the midpoint between the two.

Although the focus of most of the work on these thresholds has been on European countries, Danziger, van der Gaag, Taussig, and Smolensky (1984) applied the methodology to the United States. In this study, the authors relied on the following question: Living where you do now and meeting the expenses you consider necessary, what would be the very smallest income you (and your family) would need to make ends meet? Because the resulting subjective poverty threshold estimates lie between absolute and relative thresholds, the Leyden approach is frequently taken as providing reasonable approximations of what society deems minimum necessary incomes. This approach also has some disturbing properties, however.

One of the most notable features of subjective assessments is that they differ by gender. Men report higher income needs than absolute measures would indicate necessary, whereas women report lower income require-ments.[5] Although the goal of subjective thresholds is to estimate peoples' perceptions of economic deprivation, a gender difference in perception of needs is unlikely to reflect actual differences.

Furthermore, it would be extremely difficult to justify transfer pay-ments to one group over another simply because one group *reports* higher levels of economic need—without documentation of the form these needs take. In addition, given the difficulties inherent in phrasing survey ques-tions to ensure consistent interpretation, the results would remain suspect. Subjective poverty thresholds may be a middle ground between absolute and relative measures, but they tend to capture an element of psychological well-being and perhaps societally based expectations in addition to eco-nomic well-being.

SUMMARY

Which of the preceding definitions is the most useful in identifying poor consumers? Assuming that the goal is to identify those facing severe limitations on purchasing power and with little discretionary income, absolute measures such as those used in the United States seem the most appropriate. Absolute thresholds increase with family size and take into account the basic requirements that must be met for survival. Although relative measures offer a better picture of the disadvantage of the poorest members of society relative to the rest of society and subjective assessments capture a large component of psychological well-being, both are less accurate in identifying those with limited command over goods and services. By adjusting for needs rather than imposing an arbitrary constant income cutoff across all family sizes, we are able to identify those having the most difficult time meeting their needs in the marketplace.

AVAILABLE RESOURCES

Once a set of poverty thresholds is agreed on, the next step in measuring poverty is to assess the resources consumers have available to meet economic requirements. When marketers consider poor households as a marketing segment, they generally use annual cash income as the basis for segmentation. This basis inaccurately measures the purchasing power of poor households. Money income is not the only source of purchasing power available to families, as some poor families also receive noncash government transfers such as food stamps and housing aid. In addition, poor families frequently face tax liabilities. Consequently, annual pretax money income paints an inaccurate portrait of the poor consumer.

The Consumer Expenditure Survey (CEX) documents the difference between annual cash incomes and purchasing power. CEX publications report that consumer units (which are similar to households) with average pretax cash incomes below $5,000 have average total annual expenditures of $11,573. Using official poverty income definitions, the official poverty population reported an average level of expenditures 129% greater than their pretax cash income in 1989.[6] The following sections examine potential sources of the discrepancy between income and expenditures.

IN-KIND TRANSFERS

Cash aid (such as General Assistance and AFDC payments) represented 26.2% of total government aid to the poor in 1990. The balance of government aid to the poor takes the form of in-kind transfers, or noncash

TABLE 3.1　Cash and Noncash Income for Persons With Limited Incomes

	Expenditures, 1990	
	Dollar Amount (millions)	Percentage of Total
Total	$210,630	100
Cash aid	$55,136	26.2
Medical care	$86,197	40.9
Food benefits	$22,257	10.6
Housing benefits	$17,544	8.3
Education	$14,375	6.8
Services	$5,801	2.8
Jobs and training	$4,215	2.0
Energy assistance	$1,802	0.9

SOURCE: *Statistical Abstract of the United States* (1992, Table 565).

payments. The major in-kind transfers to poor people from the government are food stamps, school lunches, housing subsidies, and Medicare and Medicaid payments. In addition, employer contributions to health insurance also qualify as in-kind transfers. In Table 3.1, we summarize government expenditures for some of these programs in 1990. In-kind transfers accounted for more than $155 billion in aid to the poor over and above cash contributions to income. Not all of these government expenditures contribute to the purchasing power of poor consumers, as the estimates include administrative cost. Cash income clearly understates the ability of the poor to consume goods and services, however.

There is considerable debate over how to estimate the value *to* the poor of in-kind transfers such as food stamps, housing aid, and medical care. Food stamps serve as an example of the difficulty inherent in estimating the fair market value of in-kind transfers. Estimates by the U.S. Bureau of the Census consider the face value of food stamps as fair market value. An alternative assessment of the value of food stamps would decrease or discount their face value the amount by which they exceed what a comparable family would have voluntarily spent on food (Smeeding, 1977). Applying this approach, Smeeding (1977) estimated that a face dollar's worth of food stamps was worth $0.88 to recipients in 1972. Anecdotal evidence to support this discounting is reports of sales of food stamps by the poor for as low as 50 cents on the dollar.

Although maximum monthly food stamp benefits averaged around $350 in the 48 contiguous states in 1990, few households received this maximum amount. Because food stamp benefits depend on a household's size, net monthly income, and a state's maximum benefit level, it is difficult to accurately characterize benefit levels. A rough approximation, controlling for such factors, is that the average face value of a monthly benefit was $59 per person and about $150 per household in 1990 (U.S. House of Representatives, Committee on Ways and Means, 1991). Applying Smeeding's (1977) discounting factor to these amounts yields an average market value of about $51 per month for persons and $132 dollars per month for households.

Determining the value of housing aid is more complex. The U.S. Bureau of the Census relies on regression models specific to region of residence and income levels. It regresses gross rents on (a) number of bathrooms, (b) number of appliances, (c) number of housing flaws, and (d) the presence of satisfactory neighborhood services. The actual rent paid is subtracted from the predicted gross rent generated from these models for estimates of the value of the public housing subsidy.[7] The U.S. Bureau of the Census estimates that rental assistance for two-bedroom apartments for households with annual incomes less than $10,000 averaged about $220 per month. Smeeding (1977) estimated the market value of a dollar's worth of housing subsidy at $0.56 for the recipients. Using Smeeding's factor together with U.S. Bureau of the Census estimates, there is an average monthly market value of $125 per month of rental assistance to those receiving such assistance.

Medicaid and Medicare are valued at their fungible value by the U.S. Bureau of the Census—that is, they are counted as income to the extent that they free up resources that could have otherwise been spent on medical care. In 1992, the dollar value of medical benefits paid on behalf of the poorest 20% of households (those with money income less than $12,691) averaged $3,924.[8] The fungible value of the benefits averages $1,914 in employer-provided health insurance, $294 in Medicare payments, and $616 in Medicaid payments for recipients. Although these remain substantial amounts, it is difficult to argue that illness and the resulting Medicaid or Medicare expenditures make a family better off.

In summary, in-kind transfers account for a considerable percentage of the government's aid to the poor and increase poor consumers' purchasing power. They added about $2,000 of purchasing power to the average poor family's purchasing power in 1992.[9] In-kind transfers must be included as a component of income to accurately characterize the purchasing power

TABLE 3.2 Percentage Distribution of Financial Asset Holdings by Income
Category, 1984

Monthly Income as a Percentage of Poverty Line	No Assets	$1- $1,000	$1,000- $3,000	$3,000- $10,000	$10,000- $100,000	More Than $100,000
Under 100	55.3	25.1	6.7	5.9	6.6	0.4
100-150	33.2	34.4	11.9	10.6	9.5	0.5
150-200	22.2	36.2	14.0	12.5	14.8	0.4
200-300	13.7	33.4	17.3	15.8	19.0	0.9
U.S. total	19.6	25.4	14.2	16.2	22.1	2.5

SOURCE: Ruggles (1990, p. 152). Reprinted with permission of the Urban Institute.

and the level of economic deprivation of the poverty population. Most
important, marketers would be wise to recognize that poor consumers
defined in terms of cash income have more purchasing power than levels
of cash income might indicate.

ASSETS

Although assets such as houses are not included in annual incomes, they
clearly increase potential purchasing power, because they increase a consumer's ability to borrow and may be sold. Approximately 45% of the
poverty population holds positive gross assets (Ruggles, 1990).[10] Table
3.2 summarizes the 1984 distribution of gross wealth holdings as estimated by Ruggles (1990). Although more than 80% of the poverty
population held less than $1,000 of assets in 1984, 12.6% held $1,000 to
$10,000, and 7% held more than $10,000.

The effect of these asset holdings on the income of the poverty
population was estimated to decrease the number of people entering
poverty by a third (Ruggles & Williams, 1989). Not surprising, the
decrease is larger for the elderly (more than 50% fewer) than for children
because the elderly hold more assets. Because some assets are highly liquid,
some proportion of asset holdings of the poverty population should be
taken into account when estimating purchasing power. Ruggles and
Williams's (1989) estimates should be taken as an upper bound, however,
as they transformed assets to purchasing power on a dollar-for-dollar basis.
At the other extreme, the U.S. Bureau of the Census ignores all assets

TABLE 3.3 Relationship Between Income Tax Threshold and Poverty Level for a Family of Four, 1980-1990

Year	Income Tax Threshold	Poverty Level	Tax Threshold as a Percentage of Poverty Level
1980	$8,626	$8,414	102.5
1981	8,634	9,287	93.0
1982	8,727	9,862	88.5
1983	8,783	10,178	86.3
1984	8,783	10,610	82.8
1986	9,575	11,203	85.5
1987	13,288	11,611	114.4
1988	15,110	12,092	125.0
1989	15,656	12,675	123.5
1990	16,296	13,186	123.6

SOURCE: U.S. House of Representatives, Committee on Ways and Means (1991, Table 7, p. 1273).
NOTE: Tax thresholds assume full use of the earned income tax credit. The poverty-level figures are for all families, not just those with heads under age 65.

except housing. The U.S. Bureau of the Census identifies the net equity of householders in their home and applies a market rate of interest to impute an income stream. The effect of these estimates is to increase the resources of homeowners in the poorest 20% of households by an average of $1,770 (U.S. Bureau of the Census, 1993b).

TAXES

Whereas in-kind transfers and assets increase the purchasing power of the poverty population, taxes decrease it. Several different taxes affect the resources of the poverty population. To understand the effects of these taxes on poverty-level resources, it is helpful to note how they have changed over time. Table 3.3 provides a brief history of the relationship between federal income taxes and poverty thresholds between 1980 and 1990.

From 1959 to 1975, a family of four with income equal to the poverty line was obligated to pay income taxes. Following the enactment of the Earned Income Tax Credit (EITC) in 1975, such a family was not liable for federal income tax again until 1981. Starting in 1981, however, the federal income tax threshold once again crossed the poverty threshold and poverty incomes were subject to federal income taxes. The percentage of income subject to federal income tax increased until 1984, when it reached a maximum of 17.2% for such a family. The Tax Reform Act of 1986 increased the threshold for paying income taxes, and beginning in 1987, the federal income tax rate for poor families with children was effectively set equal to zero. Families with poverty-level incomes may still pay other federal taxes. For example, According to the House Ways and Means Committee, federal payroll taxes together with federal income taxes impose a 2.3% marginal tax rate on a family of four with poverty-level income; this rate increases to 4.7% and 6.1% for families of five and six, respectively (U.S. House of Representatives, Committee on Ways and Means, 1991, Table 8, p. 1275).

The impact of state income and sales taxes are more difficult to assess because they vary by state of residence. Estimates of the percentage of income paid in taxes in 1988 by a poor family of four range from a low of 0% in New Hampshire to a high of 5.3% in Missouri. The average state tax burden is 3.15% for a family of four living at the edge of poverty.

In sum, a poor family of four pays about 5% of its income in federal and state income and payroll taxes. In addition, these families also pay sales taxes and a significant proportion (about 35%) pay property taxes as well. The resources of the poorest 20% of households in 1992 were decreased by approximately $100 by taxes net of the EITC. The U.S. Bureau of the Census recognizes the significance of taxes to poverty-level incomes and estimates the effects of (a) federal income taxes, (b) state income taxes, (c) property taxes, and (d) payroll taxes.[11]

SUMMARY

The impacts of in-kind transfers and assets are summarized in Table 3.4. In-kind transfers added approximately $2,000 to the annual purchasing power of all the households living in poverty in 1992. If the imputed value of housing as an asset is included, annual resources are increased an additional $642.[12]

Using annual income as a proxy for purchasing power understated purchasing power by approximately $2,500 per poverty household in 1992. Clearly, not all individuals with low annual incomes should be considered disadvantaged as consumers. Wealthy retirees, for example, report low annual earnings but yield significant purchasing power through

TABLE 3.4 Net Effect of Noncash Items on Purchasing Power of Poor Consumers

	Average Payment to Recipients	Percentage of Poverty Households Receiving Benefit	Average Payment per Poverty Household
Food stamps	$1,764	43.9	$774
Housing assistance	2,503	19.6	491
School lunches	599	26.9	161
Employer health insurance	1,914	8.5	163
Medicare	294	31.6	93
Medicaid	616	48.3	298
Total	7,690	not available	1,980
Assets (housing)[a]	1,770	36	642
Total[b]	9,460	not available	2,622

SOURCE: U.S. Bureau of the Census (1993a, various tables).
a. The entries for housing are for the poorest 20% of households, not the official poverty population.
b. This total includes imputed income streams to home ownership for the poorest 20% of the population and therefore is only an approximation of the value to the official poverty population.

asset holdings. Furthermore, for those with few or no asset holdings, government in-kind transfers add significantly to their ability to meet their needs in the marketplace. Defining the poor solely in terms of annual cash incomes ignores radically different levels of available purchasing power and distorts the portrait of the poor consumer. Firms that specifically include or exclude poor consumers as potential customers usually use annual cash income alone as a basis for identifying these customers. As indicated in this chapter, a sole reliance on income underestimates both the size and the market potential of poor consumers.

LENGTH OF TIME IN POVERTY AND ITS EFFECT ON ESTIMATES OF MARKET POTENTIAL OF THE POOR

Most definitions of poverty rely on annual income because that information is readily available. The choice of an annual time frame for poverty definition influences the number and estimated purchasing power of poor consumers. An annual time frame does not account for the fact that a substantial portion of the poverty population is poor for a brief period of time and is able to draw on savings during periods of low income. For this reason, it is important for marketers to consider how long a household tends to be in poverty.

To assess the typical amount of time a household spends in poverty, that is, the *poverty spell length,* a distinction must be drawn between new entrants to poverty and the poverty population as a whole. New entrants to poverty consist of two types of households: those that for a variety of reasons may be expected to be poor for an extended period and those whose incomes have temporarily decreased and therefore expect a shorter stay in poverty. The most disadvantaged households stay in poverty longer and consequently make up a larger portion of the poverty population over time than those who are briefly poor. Although approximately one half of poverty *starts* last less than one year, the average spell length of the poverty population is appreciably longer.

Bane and Ellwood (1986) estimated the relative spell lengths for new entrants to poverty as well as for the poverty population as a whole using annual income data from the Panel Study of Income Dynamics (PSID) from 1970 to 1982. They estimated that of all households starting a poverty spell, 44.5% exit poverty within one year. For those households remaining in poverty after one year, the probability of their leaving falls to 28.5% the second year of their stay. The probability of leaving poverty continues to decrease as the number of years in poverty increases. This is why the average spell length of poverty for the poverty population is greater than the average spell length for all people ever entering poverty. As Bane and Ellwood (1986) noted, "Most people who are ever poor have short spells. Most people who are just beginning a spell of poverty will have a short spell. But the bulk of those poor at a given time and the bulk of the person-years of poverty are accounted for by the long-term poor" (p. 13).

Even though nearly 45% of new poverty spells last less than 1 year, and 70% are over within 3 years, Bane and Ellwood estimate the average length of a stay in poverty for new entrants as 4.2 years. Spell length for the currently poor averages 12.3 years due to the gradual selection of the more disadvantaged households among the poor. The distinction between the spell lengths of new entrants to poverty and the poverty population as a whole is relevant to the difference in purchasing power between the transitory and the persistently poor.

Government and business rely on annual income in defining poverty and the character of spell lengths. Some of those who are temporarily poor

TABLE 3.5 The Persistently Poor—Alternative Definitions

Author(s)	Definition	Percentage of Official Poverty Population
Levy (1977)	In poverty 5 of 7 years between 1967 and 1973	40%-45% of 1967 base
Coe (1978)	In poverty every year between 1967 and 1975	12% of 1976 base
Hill (1981)	In poverty 8 of 10 years between 1969 and 1978	20%-25% of 1978 base
Hill (1981)	In poverty every year 1969 to 1975	6% of 1978 base
Duncan, Coe, & Hill (1984)	In poverty 8 or more years between 1969 and 1978	20%-25% of 1978 base

SOURCE: Ruggles (1990, Table 5.7, pp. 107-108). Reprinted with permission of the Urban Institute.

may not decrease their consumer expenditures on a dollar-to-dollar basis with their decrease in income, however. People who fall into poverty for short periods may solve their short-term fall in income by drawing on savings or accumulating debt. Although there are no data available on the borrowing patterns, including installment debt, of the poverty population, it stands to reason that this is an avenue for the short-term poor to meet their obligations. This issue is discussed in more detail in Chapter 6. Furthermore, whatever credit is available to the poverty population represents purchasing power. Consequently, for this subgroup of short-term poor, annual income serves as a poor proxy for purchasing power. Nonetheless, it should be recognized that, as noted by Ruggles and Williams (1989), "Most of those with poverty spells have relatively low incomes over longer periods, making it unlikely that they would be able to borrow without much collateral" (p. 235).

What about the persistently poor, the consumers with the most limited purchasing power? Estimates of the number of persistently poor vary due to the different definitions employed. Table 3.5 summarizes some of the research on this topic. The persistently poor account for 6% to 45% of the total poverty population depending on the definition employed.

The distinction between people who are poor for short and for long periods of time should alert marketers to a bias inherent in using data about consumer behavior collected on an annual basis. Annual data tend to obscure the difference between temporarily poor and more permanently poor households. The former are likely to have more resources than the latter for purchasing discretionary products and services, for purchasing more costly goods, and for purchasing larger quantities. Again, income alone is inadequate as a basis for segmenting poor households.

Both transitory and persistently poor consumers have long-term value for marketers. Furthermore, the majority of the poverty population faces a limited stay in poverty. Because their stay in poverty is limited, they are potentially more profitable consumers in the future. As marketers have found with the general population, brand building is essential to profitability, and it is less expensive to keep a customer than to gain a new customer, hence, the current emphasis on marketing for building relationships with customers. Furthermore, the transitory poor often remain as customers for many products and brands even while they are in a state of poverty and are worth keeping as customers. For these reasons, it is worth expending marketing time and resources to build brand equity and usage among poor consumers. Efforts to do so should pay off faster for the transitory poor but should be profitable for both groups.

SUMMARY AND IMPLICATIONS

We have argued that using arbitrary income cutoffs to identify poor consumers not only ignores the substantial academic literature but also yields an inappropriate definition of poor consumers. Starting with the proposition that poor consumers are those with the most limited ability to meet their economic requirements in the marketplace, we urge consideration of three factors to better capture such consumers.

First, an accounting of economic requirements must be made. Simple income cutoffs that ignore differences in levels of economic need do not accurately capture those individuals and families with the most difficult time meeting their needs in the marketplace. In particular, such simple cutoffs categorize too many individuals and small families and too few large families as poor consumers. Although a number of approaches are possible for a needs accounting, adoption of the official U.S. poverty thresholds offers the most appropriate and simple solution. Not only do the official poverty thresholds account for differences in economic requirements for different family sizes, but they also are widely accepted and readily available to analysts interested in identifying poor consumers.

Second, we have argued that pretax cash income serves as a poor measure of purchasing power for poor consumers. It is clear that in-kind transfers, assets, and taxes cause cash income to understate purchasing power. Ideally, an explicit accounting should be made of these factors, but this is not always possible with available data. Nonetheless, recognition of the understatement should lead marketers to conclude that people with low cash incomes frequently enjoy purchasing power in excess of their reported incomes. Furthermore, inclusion of such noncash income amounts will change the composition of the population of poor consumers—a topic we discuss in the following chapter.

Finally, the use of annual income also acts to misportray poor consumers. Although the poverty population is poor an average of more than 12 years, it is also true that the average length of stay in poverty of those just entering poverty averages just over 4 years. Even though distinguishing between short-term and long-term poor consumers may not be possible because of lack of data, marketers who appreciate the dynamics of poverty spell lengths will be better able to identify the different needs and abilities of both the short-term and long-term poor population.

APPENDIX: POVERTY THRESHOLDS

The official U.S. poverty thresholds are based on the work of M. Orshansky (1963, 1965, 1969). As noted previously, she adopted an absolute approach in her development of poverty thresholds. She noted the difficulty inherent in establishing needs standards but stated that, "if it is not possible to state unequivocally 'how much is enough,' it should be possible to assert with confidence how much, on average, is too little" (1965, p. 3). She took several steps in developing the poverty thresholds.

The first step was to estimate the dollar amount required to meet the U.S. Department of Agriculture's (USDA) economy and low-cost food plans. The low-cost plan was based on the food consumption patterns of the poorest third of the income distribution and had been used previously by welfare agencies to determine food allotments. The economy food plan was set at 75% to 80% of the low-cost food plan and was designated by the USDA as being appropriate for temporary or emergency use when funds were low. The food plans provided estimates of the nutritional needs for individuals across 19 age classes and Orshansky assigned food costs according to family composition, that is, for variety of family sizes, number of children, age of household head, and farm status. Some of the adjustments were admittedly ad hoc, due to data limitations, for example, and as Orshansky stressed, there was little control made for the ages of children within the family even though food requirements for children advance rapidly with age. The next step in the procedure was to estimate the percentage of income that should be allocated to food expenditures.

The third step was to establish an income multiplier to apply to food expenditures. The results of a 1955 USDA study (U.S. Department of Health Education and Welfare, 1976) of family food consumption and dietary adequacy found that nonfarm families spent 27% to 46% of their income on food. Orshansky took these estimates and those from a 1961 Bureau of Labor Statistics study (U.S. Department of Health Education and Welfare, 1976) focusing on urban families (which reported 25% of income spent on food) and conjectured that the average nonfarm family spent one third of its income on food. A further adjustment was made for farm families. The USDA had estimated that 40% of all food items consumed by farm families came from their home farm or garden. Accordingly, it was assumed that a farm family would need 40% less net cash than a nonfarm family of the same size and composition. Two sets of poverty thresholds were then developed by taking the economy and low-cost food plans and multiplying them by three.

The Office of Economic Opportunity unofficially adopted the low-cost thresholds in May 1965. By 1969, after extensive discussions, two changes were made to the thresholds: The farm thresholds were set at 85% of the nonfarm thresholds rather than the original 60%, and the Consumer Price Index was made the basis for the annual adjustment for the poverty thresholds rather than the annual change in the per capita cost of food in the economy food plan (Fisher, 1992). In August 1969, the Bureau of the Budget directed all federal executive branch agencies to use the thresholds, making them the official poverty thresholds for the United States. Aside from the annual price adjustments, there have been two sets of revisions in the poverty thresholds since their official adoption.

In 1979, the poverty thresholds were updated using a new price index, the Consumer Price Index for All Urban Consumers (CPI-U). In 1981, three additional revisions were made: (a) the farm/nonfarm differential was eliminated, (b) the matrix of poverty thresholds was extended to make the largest family size nine or more rather than seven or more, and (c) the distinction for gender of family head was eliminated. These are the last set of revisions made and the current poverty thresholds equal the 1981 thresholds plus an inflation factor measured by the CPI-U. Table 3.6 presents the matrix of poverty thresholds for 1992.

Although there have been no revisions in the poverty thresholds since 1981, except for annual cost of living adjustments, there has been considerable debate regarding their revision.

At the request of Congress, the Committee on National Statistics of the National Academy of Sciences began a 30-month study in early 1992 to evaluate alternative definitions of poverty. Two major sets of issues were to be addressed by this body. One relates to the measurement of income and available resources, and the other relates to the poverty thresholds themselves. The discussions on available resources focus on the issues highlighted in this chapter—how to best control for taxes, in-kind transfers, and assets. The discussion on the thresholds themselves focuses on the possibility of updating the thresholds to account for changes in consumption patterns, better assessments of equivalency scales across family types and sizes, and variations in the cost of living.

The published report of recommendations (National Research Council, 1995) suggests several revisions to the current poverty thresholds and the calculation of poverty. Broadly speaking, the poverty threshold would change from an absolute threshold to a quasi-relative threshold. In brief, the council suggests that consumer expenditure data be used to calculate the amount spent on food, clothing, and shelter (including utilities) for families at the 30th percentile of expenditures for two-parent/two-child families and that this amount be adjusted for differences in family size. The basic poverty thresholds should then be set at 1.15 to 1.25 times this amount. Furthermore, adjustments should be made in housing costs for nine census regions and for different metropolitan population sizes based on U.S. Bureau of the Census calculations.

In addition, the council suggests that resources should be defined, "as the sum of money income from all sources together with the value of near-money benefits (e.g., food stamps) that are available to buy goods and services in the budget, minus expenses that cannot be used to buy these goods and services" (National Research Council, 1995, p. 5). In particular, the proposed revisions would exclude taxes, out-of-pocket health care expenditures, child care, and work expenses. Adoption of these proposed changes is uncertain; it should be noted that the council's report

TABLE 3.6 Poverty Thresholds by Size of Family and Number of Related Children Under 18 Years, 1992

	Weighted Average	0	1	2	3	4	5	6	7	8 or more
One person	$7,143									
Under 65	7,299	7,299								
65 +	6,729	6,729								
Two persons	9,137									
Head < 65	9,443	9,395	9,670							
Head 65 +	8,487	8,480	9,634							
Three persons	11,186	10,974	11,293	11,304						
Four persons	14,335	14,471	14,708	14,228	14,277					
Five persons	16,592	17,452	17,705	17,163	16,743	16,487				
Six persons	19,137	20,072	20,152	19,737	19,339	18,747	18,396			
Seven persons	21,594	23,096	23,240	22,743	22,396	21,751	20,998	20,171		
Eight persons	24,053	25,831	26,059	25,590	25,179	24,596	23,855	23,085	22,889	
Nine or more	28,745	31,073	31,223	30,808	30,459	29,887	29,099	28,387	28,211	27,124

SOURCE: U.S. Bureau of the Census (1993b).

was not unanimously supported within the council itself and includes an appendix containing statement of dissent by councilmember John Cogan.

NOTES

1. This figure was based on a consensus within the CEA and drew on work performed by Orshansky (1963) and Robert Lampmann, then a member of the CEA staff. In 1994 dollars, this translates into $14,700 for families of two or more and $7,350 for singles. (Although reported in 1964, the amounts were expressed in 1962 dollars.)

2. Average family income in 1990 for unrelated individuals, families of two, three, four, and five or more are $18,678, $32,790, $37,719, $43,545, and $40,602, respectively (*Statistical Abstract of the United States*, 1992, Table 692).

3. It might possibly increase at a decreasing rate but not actually fall.

4. The theoretical foundation was developed by researchers from the Leyden Income Evaluation Project (see Goedhart, Halberstadt, Kapteyn, & Van Praag, 1977).

5. Danziger et al. (1984) report that based on subjective assessments the poverty rate for nonaged white males would increase about 40% whereas the poverty rate for aged white females would fall by more than 50%.

6. Based on calculations by one of the authors using 1989 CEX interview data, average pretax income of the poverty population was $5,483 and average total expenditures were $12,553.

7. These estimates do not coincide with the face value of housing vouchers, as the vouchers are typically set equal to the difference between market rent and 30% of a family's income.

8. On average, Medicare accounted for $1,561, Medicaid for $1,065, and health insurance supplements to wage and salary income contributed $1,298 (U.S. Bureau of the Census, 1993a, Table 1, pp. 2-3).

9. Calculation based on U.S. Bureau of the Census (1993a, Table 7).

10. Her estimates were based on data from the 1984 Survey of Income and Program Participation (SIPP).

11. The calculations are based on an expansion of the Annual Demographic data files (the March Current Population Survey) that simulate tax-filing status, adjusted gross income, capital gains, and other items through a matching process with Internal Revenue Service data.

12. These estimates probably overstate the increase in purchasing power because food stamps are taken at face value, and Medicare and Medicaid payments may not be used for other goods or services. The value of Medicare and Medicaid, although presented at their fungible value, are paid to households with medically needy members, which offsets some of the increased economic welfare.

4

The Poverty Population

You have no savings, no emergency funds, you don't take vacations,
you don't put money away for retirement and you reach retirement
with absolutely no benefits.

—Cicily Maton, quoted in
Longworth and Stein (1995, p. 6)[1]

To appreciate the problems of poor consumers in the marketplace, we
must place a face on poor people. Public perceptions of the poverty
population are frequently inaccurate, and these misconceptions can lead
to poor marketing decisions and public policy. In this chapter, we describe
the poverty population in some detail to focus the debate on the needs of
poor consumers. Although we made clear in Chapter 3 that there is no
perfect definition of poverty, we rely in this chapter on the official U.S.
definition. Although the shortcomings of this approach have been noted,
it is the most appropriate method for identifying consumers who face the
most difficulty meeting their needs in the marketplace—poor consumers.

We begin with a presentation of poverty trends for both families and
individuals in the United States. Because resources are commonly shared
in families and therefore most consumption decisions are made at the
family level, family poverty statistics capture the concept of the consumer
unit. Not all persons live in families, however. The U.S. Bureau of the
Census excludes single individuals living alone or with other unrelated

individuals from its definition of *family*. Consequently, person-level data paint a more complete picture of consumer units and the residents of the poverty population.

In our discussion of trends in poverty rates, we highlight the difference between two important numbers, the incidence of poverty for demographic groups and the percentage of the poverty population accounted for by particular groups. Confusion between rates of incidence and the composition of the poverty population frequently lead to the incorrect impression that the majority of the poverty population is made up of minorities in single-parent families. It is not. Although the poverty population does not represent the overall U.S. population, it is a diverse group.

Poverty is obviously related to a lack of income, but people become poor for various reasons. In the next section of this chapter, we summarize some of the most common reasons that families and individuals begin a spell of poverty. One of the most important observations is that although starts are indeed frequently due to decreases in income, for some demographic groups a change in family composition is the primary catalyst for poverty spells.

In the third section of this chapter, we identify the effects of different measures of income on the level of poverty in the United States. In the previous chapter, we noted the additional purchasing power due to in-kind transfers and assets for poor people. In this section, we estimate the impact these additions have on the size of the poverty population. In the final section of this chapter, we review some behavioral aspects of the poor population that may influence consumption decisions.

TRENDS IN POVERTY

Poverty rates are most commonly reported for families and persons. The poverty rates for the two groups need not be the same, as unrelated individuals are excluded from family poverty rates. Figure 4.1 summarizes the trends in poverty for persons and families between 1959 and 1992.

In 1992, the poverty rate was 14.5%—the highest since the 1982-1983 time period and a rate that had not been seen prior to that since 1966. As Figure 4.1 demonstrates, poverty rates varied widely between 1959 and 1992. They fell throughout the 1960s, increased in 1970, then continued

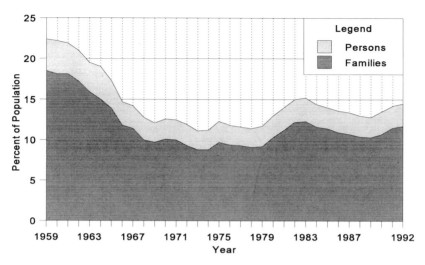

Figure 4.1. Poverty Rate, 1959-1992
SOURCE: U.S. Bureau of the Census (1993b).

their decline, albeit at a much slower rate, between 1971 and 1973. The rates rose again in 1974 and 1975 and then began a gradual decline from 1976 to 1978. Starting in 1979, poverty rates increased for 5 consecutive years before starting to decline again in 1985. This decline lasted until 1990.

POOR FAMILIES

Table 4.1 summarizes the rates of poverty for different family types between 1973 and 1992.[2] Although poverty rates were at historic lows in 1973, they declined for every year on record prior to 1973 with the exception of 1970. Consequently, 1973 serves as a convenient breaking point for analysis. Although the trends in family poverty rates are similar across race of head of household and family type, there are clear differences in the incidence of poverty. Families headed by African Americans are most prone to live in poverty, followed by those headed by Hispanics. Families headed by Whites have a significantly lower probability of being poor. The probability of living in poverty for a member of a White-headed family was less than one third that of a member of an African-American-headed family in 1992 (8.9% compared to 30.9%). Family type also plays

TABLE 4.1 Poverty Rates for Families

Year	All	White	African American	Hispanic	Married Couples	Single Female With Children
1973	8.8	6.6	28.1	19.8	5.3	43.2
1975	9.7	7.7	27.1	25.1	6.1	44.0
1977	9.3	7.0	28.2	21.4	5.3	41.8
1979	9.2	6.9	27.8	20.3	5.4	39.6
1981	11.2	8.8	30.8	24.0	6.8	44.3
1983	12.3	9.7	32.3	25.9	7.6	47.1
1985	11.4	9.1	28.7	25.5	6.7	45.4
1987	10.7	8.1	29.4	25.5	5.8	45.5
1989	10.3	7.8	27.8	23.4	5.6	42.8
1990	10.7	8.1	29.3	25.0	5.7	44.5
1991	11.5	8.8	30.4	26.5	6.0	47.1
1992	11.7	8.9	30.9	26.2	6.2	45.7

SOURCE: U.S. Bureau of the Census (1993b).

a large role in the determination of poverty status. Married-couple families have a lower than average poverty rate, 6.2% in 1992, whereas members of female-headed families with children face almost a one in two chance of living in poverty.

Table 4.2 provides a more detailed description of the poverty population in 1992. There are three columns in this table. "Incidence" refers to the probability of a family having pretax cash income, excluding capital gains, lower than the official U.S. poverty threshold (e.g., 10.2% of families living in the Northeast region are in poverty). "Percentage of poverty population" indicates the proportion of the poverty population for each category of family (e.g., 17.2% of all families living in poverty reside in the Northeast). "Mean poverty deficit" is a measure of poverty severity and equals the average amount that a poor family's income falls below its respective poverty threshold.

To understand the poor consumer, we must appreciate the distinction between the incidence of poverty and the percentage of the poverty population. To demonstrate, look at the entries for Whites in Table 4.2. Although Whites have a much lower probability of living in poverty than African Americans or Hispanics, they make up the majority of the population and therefore account for the greatest percentage of the poor. Thus, although the incidence of poverty for Whites, at 8.9%, is lower than that of African Americans and Hispanics (30.9% and 26.2%, respec-

TABLE 4.2 Poverty Summary—Families, 1992

Group	Incidence	Percentage of Poverty Population	Mean Poverty Deficit
All families	11.7	100.0	$5,751
Race of family head			
White	8.9	64.8	$5,335
African American	30.9	30.6	$6,621
Hispanic	26.2	17.5	$5,834
Family type			
Married with children	8.4	27.2	$5,956
Female head with children	45.7	47.3	$6,520
Type of residence			
Inside metropolitan area	11.3	74.2	$5,856
Outside metropolitan area	13.0	25.8	$5,449
Region			
Northeast	10.2	17.2	$5,708
Midwest	10.2	21.0	$5,768
South	13.8	41.7	$5,849
West	11.2	20.1	$5,548
Full-time, full-year workers			
No workers	31.6	41.1	$6,045
One worker	17.6	42.3	$4,389
Two or more workers	3.4	16.6	$5,087

SOURCE: U.S. Bureau of the Census (1993b).

tively), 64.8% of the poverty population is White, 30.6% is African American, and 17.5% is Hispanic.[3] The statement that African Americans and Hispanics are more likely to live in poverty is true, but it does not follow that they typify the poverty population. Not only are families headed by African Americans more likely to live in poverty, they experience more severe poverty; they have an average poverty deficit of $6,621 compared to $5,834 for Hispanics and $5,335 for White-headed families.

Women in Poverty

Family structure is clearly an important determinant of poverty status. One of the most striking observations is that families with children make up more than three quarters of the poverty population (see Table 4.2). Female-headed families with children account for most of this group, constituting approximately one half of all families living in poverty. If families headed by women living in poverty are broken down by race, 20.8% of all poverty families are headed by African American women with children, 24.9% by White women with children, and 6.8% by Hispanic women with children. The proportion of the poverty population made up of families headed by women with children has increased over time and has attracted significant attention from public policymakers.

Why has poverty become so associated with women? The *incidence of poverty* for families headed by women has remained relatively constant over time and is not the reason for the "feminization of poverty." Rather, the feminization of poverty is driven by the increase in the *percentage* of families that are headed by women with no spouse present. The percentage of poor families headed by a woman is correlated to the steady increase since 1970 in the number of out-of-wedlock births.

Not only are families headed by women the dominant family type in the poverty population, they also are most deeply in poverty and have the highest poverty deficits. The average poverty deficit was $5,751 per family living in poverty in 1992. For families headed by women the deficit averages $6,520. Any proposals to ease the plight of poor consumers must keep the needs of this group at the forefront.

The higher poverty rate among single African American mothers is not attributable to cultural differences between African Americans and Whites. African American attitudes to family are very traditional, and most African American women would rather live in a traditional two-parent family (Nichols-Casebolt, 1988). One explanation has been that few economically stable males are available (Nichols-Casebolt, 1988; Wilson, 1987). Another possible explanation is that the relative level of a wife's income to a husband's has increased, which can cause family dissension (Farley, 1988; Nichols-Casebolt, 1988). Although a relatively higher income for women may explain low marriage and high divorce and separation rates, it does not explain the higher birth rate among African American women who never married.[4] This gap between African Americans and Whites is closing; the percentage of all live births by unwed White mothers more than tripled over the past 20 years.

Other Poor Families

The next most common type of family found in the poverty population is married couples with children. Their incidence of poverty is 8.4%, and they account for approximately 27% of the poverty population. The balance of the poor are either male-headed families with children (4.3% of the poverty population), married couples without children (14.5%), or families headed by single males and females without children under age 18 (6.8%).

Other Demographic Characteristics of Poor Families

The belief that the poor are mostly residents of the older central cities is incorrect. Families who live *outside* metropolitan areas are more prone to live in poverty than those within a metropolitan area. Because most of the U.S. population resides in metropolitan areas, however, 75% of all poverty families live inside the central city and its suburbs. It is true that the majority of poverty families live in metropolitan areas (central cities and their suburbs) and the largest portion of poverty families live in central cities (42.4%), but it is also true that the majority of poverty families reside outside the central city in the suburbs and rural areas (57.6%). Families that reside in metropolitan areas have a lower incidence of poverty, but even without controlling for the relatively higher costs of living in metropolitan areas, they have greater poverty deficits than those in outlying areas (see Table 4.2). Thus, the metropolitan poor are poorer than their rural cousins.

The largest segment of the U.S. poverty population lives in the South. The inordinately larger share of the poverty population in the South may be due to the lower cost of living in the South relative to other regions. This lower cost of living lowers wage rates but not poverty thresholds, inflating poverty rates in the South.

The majority of families living in poverty in 1992 provided one or more full-time workers who worked for the entire year. Forty percent of poor families provide no full-time year-round workers to the labor force. The issue of labor force participation is examined in more detail in the discussion of individual poverty rates.

Popular characterizations of the poor are consistent with families most at risk of living in poverty but provide an inaccurate description of the poverty population. The poverty population is diverse, so a summary of the key descriptors may be useful. The family type most commonly encountered in the poverty population is a family headed by a single mother, but the majority of poverty families (a) are headed by Whites, (b) live inside

TABLE 4.3 Poverty Rates for Persons

Year	All	White	African American	Hispanic	Elderly	Children
1973	11.1	8.4	31.4	21.9	18.6	14.4
1975	12.3	9.7	31.3	26.9	14.6	17.1
1977	11.6	8.9	30.6	22.4	15.0	16.2
1979	11.7	9.0	31.0	21.8	15.2	16.4
1981	14.0	11.1	34.2	26.5	15.3	20.0
1983	15.2	12.1	35.7	28.0	13.8	22.3
1985	14.0	11.4	31.3	29.0	12.6	20.7
1987	13.4	10.4	32.4	28.0	12.5	20.3
1989	12.8	10.0	30.7	26.2	11.4	19.6
1990	13.5	10.7	31.9	28.1	12.2	20.6
1991	14.2	11.3	32.7	28.7	12.4	21.8
1992	14.5	11.6	33.3	29.3	12.9	21.9

SOURCE: U.S. Bureau of the Census (1993b).

central cities, (c) provide one or more full-time full-year workers to the labor force, and (d) live in the southern region of the United States. Families most at risk of living in poverty (a) are minority headed, (b) are headed by single parents with children, (c) live outside central cities, and (d) do not provide any full-time, full-year workers to the labor force.

POOR PERSONS

Poverty rates among individuals highlight the rise of poverty among children in the contemporary world. To complete the description of the poverty population, Table 4.3 summarizes poverty rates for persons in select years between 1973 and 1992. Although the racial trends are similar to those reported for families, the trends in poverty for the elderly and children require additional comment. The elderly are one of the few success stories of the War on Poverty implemented under the Johnson administration. Poverty rates for the elderly fell steadily between 1973 and 1992, while all other demographic groups experienced increases in poverty. For example, children saw their probability of living in poverty increase by 50% (7.5 percentage points), and by 1992 a child had a better than one in five chance of living in poverty.[5]

As Table 4.3 makes clear, the poverty population changed composition between 1973 and 1992. In 1992, African Americans and Hispanics were

TABLE 4.4 Poverty Summary—Persons, 1992

Group	Incidence	Percentage of Poverty Population
All persons	14.5	100
Race		
White	11.6	66.5
African American	33.3	28.8
Hispanic	29.3	18.0
Age		
< 15	22.7	34.8
15-24	17.8	16.6
25-44	11.5	25.7
45-64	8.9	12.0
65+	12.9	10.8

Education (aged 25+)	Incidence	Percentage of All Poor	Percentage of Poor 25+
< High school	25.6	22.3	46.0
High school	10.4	16.2	33.5
Some college	7.0	7.1	14.6
Bachelor's degree +	3.0	2.9	5.9

Labor Force (aged 18-64)	Incidence	Percentage of All Poor	Percentage of Poor Aged 18-64
Full year/full time	2.6	5.7	11.5
Less than full year/full time	14.8	18.5	37.4
Not working	31.3	25.3	51.1

SOURCE: U.S. Bureau of the Census (1993b).

the most prone to live in poverty, as they had been in 1973, and saw their poverty rates increase, but in those 19 years children replaced the elderly as the next most prone group to live in poverty.

Over one third of persons living in poverty are less than 15 years of age—a most disturbing observation (see Table 4.4). More than one in five children under the age of 15 live in poverty. Individuals aged 45 to 64 faced the lowest incidence of poverty in 1992, and the elderly made up the smallest proportion of the poverty population. The young make up a disproportionate share of the poor in the United States. Although people under age 24 account for about 36% of the total U.S. population, they are just over one half of the poverty population.

Education

The effect of educational attainment on poverty status is dramatic. Restricting the population to those assumed to have completed their formal schooling (individuals 25 years of age or older), poverty rates fall with increased education. A high school diploma decreases the probability of living in poverty by 59% (15.2 percentage points less than high school dropouts). Having some college education decreases the incidence of poverty by an additional 30%. People who have completed college rarely live in poverty (3%). Not only do the poorly educated run a higher risk of living in poverty, almost one half of those over the age of 25 living in poverty do not have high school diplomas, and more than three quarters hold a high school diploma or less.

Working

It was noted earlier that the majority of families living in poverty provided more than one full-time full-year worker to the labor force. In fact, almost one half of the working-age poor report working *at least* part time, with fully 11.5% working full year full time. This means that about one half of the working-age poverty population did work in 1992. Look at the bottom of Table 4.4 to see labor force participation patterns for working-age people, those between the ages of 18 and 64. As one might expect, the probability of living in poverty drops with the level of labor force participation. Although 31.3% of individuals who are not working are poor, only 2.6% of those working full time for the entire year live in poverty.

The reasons given for not participating in the labor force are best examined separately by gender (see Table 4.5). For example, in 1992, 40.6% of all working-age persons who were not working and were living in poverty reported home or family reasons as the cause—they were caring for someone at home. This reason is most reported by women. More than 80% of working-age women living in poverty who do not work report other obligations (home or family reasons), medical reasons, or an inability to find work. In contrast, men's most frequent reason for not working is that they are ill or disabled or they cannot find work. Overall, about three quarters of the unemployed poor report that they do not work for one of these three reasons. Most important, after accounting for disability, lack of employment opportunities, and caretaker demands, the vast majority of the poor who are able to work do so.[6]

TABLE 4.5 Reasons for Not Working, 1992

Reason All Poor 18-64 Not Working	Percentage of	
	Those Not Working	Poverty Population
Ill or disabled	24.5	6.2
Retired	4.9	1.2
Home or family reasons	40.6	10.3
Could not find work	13.7	3.5
School or other reason	16.3	4.1
Reason Males 18-64 Not Working	Males Not Working	
Ill or disabled	38.5	3.8
Retired	6.6	0.6
Home or family reasons	4.2	0.4
Could not find work	25.6	2.5
School or other reason	25.1	2.4
Reason Females 18-64 Not Working	Females Not Working	
Ill or disabled	18.2	3.9
Retired	4.1	0.9
Home or family reasons	57.0	12.3
Could not find work	8.3	1.8
School or other reason	12.3	2.7

SOURCE: U.S. Bureau of the Census (1993b).

SUMMARY

How can the poor consumer be characterized? The poor are heterogeneous on various dimensions, such as demographics (e.g., geographic location, gender, ethnic background, age), time in poverty (less and more temporary), and causes of falling into poverty. The implication for marketers is that by being aware of the differences in demographics of the poor, they can develop and market products to suit the needs of these segments. Demographic differences among the poor also have implications for public policymakers. These differences should be included in criteria used to judge poverty and should be considered in programs to fulfill basic needs of the poor, such as food, clothing, child care, and transportation.

A large and growing portion of the poverty population consists of children living in single-parent families, typically headed by a poorly educated woman and living in a metropolitan area. Although this is an oversimplification, it is clear that any serious effort to meet the needs of poor consumers must address the needs of this group. Families with children would be expected to devote a larger portion of their income to food; child care products such as diapers, infant formula, and children's clothing; and for older children, books and school supplies. Because of the pressures of raising a child without a partner, single parents might place a high value on convenience in meeting their consumer needs. For example, transporting the children to the store is difficult even if a car is available, but using public transit to transport both children and purchases becomes quite formidable and near impossible.

To the extent that areas of concentrated poverty are underserved by retail outlets (a topic explored in Chapter 8) and that goods targeted for children are considered more profitable to marketers, most poor consumers are doubly penalized—once by their low income and again by business practices. In fact, the profit margin for retail children's clothing stores is higher (4.8) than for women's (4.0) or men's (4.2) clothing stores (Dun Analytical Services, 1994).

REASONS FOR BECOMING POOR

Poverty rates are correlated with aggregate economic activity. Poverty increases during economic recessions (Blank & Blinder, 1986; Gottschalk & Danziger, 1984). Understanding what causes a person to become poor helps us understand *who* is poor. In their analysis of the Panel Study of Income Dynamics (PSID), Bane and Ellwood (1986) isolated the primary reasons people enter poverty. Their results are summarized in Table 4.6.

The most common cause of poverty for families is a fall in the earnings of the household head, which supports the hypothesis that poverty is caused by macroeconomic conditions.[7] Bane and Ellwood estimated that 37.9% of all poverty spells beginning between 1970 and 1982 were due to a decrease in the head's earned income level. If earnings of other family members are included, approximately one half of all poverty starts can be attributed directly to decreases in earnings. This is consistent with time series data that indicate a high degree of correlation between levels of economic activity and poverty rates.

This reason for becoming poor is not true for all family types, however. Decreases in income from earnings and other sources account for approxi-

TABLE 4.6 Causes of Poverty Spell Beginnings

	All	Married Couples With Children			Female Heads With Children		Single Heads With No Children	
		Heads	Wives	Children	Heads	Children	Male	Female
Earnings decrease								
Head	37.9	58.1	57.5	57.1	14.4	14.5	32.4	24.6
Spouse	3.7	6.5	6.8	5.6	dna	dna	1.6	dna
Other member	7.7	4.5	4.7	4.9	10.1	14.0	3.5	8.1
Total	49.3	69.1	69.0	67.6	24.5	28.5	37.5	32.7
Other income fell	8.0	4.6	7.0	6.1	9.7	11.0	4.3	9.9
Increase in needs	8.2	15.7	8.7	10.9	7.1	7.6	3.8	0.7
Child forms a family	14.7	10.6	13.4	dna	20.7	dna	54.5	41.9
Loss of male head	15.0	dna	1.9	1.5	38.3	33.9	dna	14.8
Child born into poverty	8.6	dna	dna	13.8	dna	19.0	dna	dna
Percentage of total	100.0	8.8	9.5	26.4	8.1	17.8	7.3	9.8

SOURCE: Adapted by Bane and Ellwood (1986). Reprinted with permission of the University of Wisconsin Press.

mately three fourths of poverty starts for married couples with children and more than one half of poverty starts in the aggregate, but decreases in income are less important for other family types.

For people in families headed by women (and for unrelated individuals), the most common cause of a spell in poverty is a change in family status. Family dissolution, through death, divorce, or separation, leads to about 15% of all poverty starts. More striking, it accounts for about one third of starts for families headed by women.[8] The next most common cause of poverty for women is the start of a new family unit (e.g., a child moving out of the house and beginning a family). New family formation, either through dissolution of an existing family or through the creation of a new family causes over one half of all poverty starts for single-parent-headed households. Also, these reasons account for more than 50% of new beginnings for single household heads with no children.

In summary, both economic forces and demographic factors play roles in causing poverty. Although decreases in earnings are more important for married couples with children, for families headed by single persons, changes in family status are the primary cause of entering poverty. Knowing that a key reason for poverty is new household formation is a trigger for recognizing a marketing opportunity for businesses. New households need a variety of basic goods and services. Even if newly formed households

TABLE 4.7 Average Income and Expenditures, 1989

Poverty Definition	Average Income	Average Expenditures	Poverty Rate
Pretax cash income	$5,483	$12,553	15.1%
Pretax cash income and total expenditures	$5,807	$6,641	7.1%

furnish with used goods, they represent return business when they up-
grade to new furnishings.

POVERTY, MEASURES OF INCOME,
AND PURCHASING POWER

As described in Chapter 3, annual cash income is a poor proxy for
purchasing power, and poverty rates are sensitive to the definition of
income employed in their calculation. In Table 4.7, we present summary
statistics on the average expenditure levels and incomes of the official
poverty population to support this contention.[9] Figures are reported for
two populations in Table 4.7, those officially poor and those with both
incomes and total expenditures below the poverty threshold. The officially
defined poor reported an average of approximately $7,000 more in
expenditures than annual before-tax income in 1989. In fact, more than
one half of the families classified as "income poor" report expenditure
levels in excess of the poverty threshold. As we shall see in Chapter 5, the
poor are cautious shoppers, so their expenditures in excess of reported
income are likely to be necessary. As noted by Donley (1994), if the
poverty population is restricted to those holding income *and* reporting
consumption below the poverty threshold, the poverty rate is cut in half.
The ability to spend more than you make cannot be sustained over time,
however, and these people are at high risk.

Why are expenditures so much higher than cash income for the official
poverty population? One explanation concerns the way the poverty rate
is calculated. The official poverty rates in the United States are based on
annual pretax cash income, excluding capital gains income, but the U.S.
Bureau of the Census does calculate alternative poverty statistics. Table
4.8 summarizes poverty rates in the United States for 1992 for several

TABLE 4.8 Poverty Rates by Income Definition, 1992

Income Definition	Percentage of	
	Families	Persons
Cash income excluding capital gains = (1)	11.7	14.5
(1) – Government transfers = (2)	20.1	22.6
(2) + Capital gains = (3)	20.0	22.5
(3) + Health supplements to earned income = (4)	19.5	21.9
(4) – Taxes net of the EITC = (5)	19.9	22.6
(5) + Cash transfers = (6)	11.5	14.4
(6) + Medicare = (7)	11.1	14.0
(7) + Medicaid = (8)	10.3	13.0
(8) + Other noncash transfers = (9)	9.2	11.7
(9) + Return on own homes = (10)	8.2	10.4

SOURCE: U.S. Bureau of the Census (1993a).

income definitions. As was noted previously, official poverty rates were 14.5% for all persons and 11.7% for all families in 1992. Taxes and government transfers alter purchasing power substantially, however. For example, excluding government cash transfers to the poor increases poverty rates to 22.6% and 20.1% for persons and families, respectively. Government taxes, net of the Earned Income Tax Credit (EITC), increase the levels of poverty. Medicare, Medicaid, and other noncash transfers decrease poverty rates to 11.7% and 9.2% for persons and families, respectively. Adding the return from owned homes decreases the rate to 10.4% for persons and 8.2% of families.

A second explanation for the difference between expenditures and annual incomes relies on the *permanent income hypothesis:* Consumers base consumption decisions on their permanent income rather than their current or observed income. Permanent income can be thought of as the stable portion of income after controlling for random shocks. Permanent and current income differ due to transitory changes in income that may be positive or negative. Transitory changes in income, due to temporary unemployment or illness, do not alter permanent income and therefore should not decrease annual expenditures. With a temporary decrease in income, families borrow against future income or draw down savings from previous periods and their expenditure levels remain relatively unscathed.

A third possible explanation is the *life cycle theory* of consumption: Consumption is smoothed over an individual's lifetime. Earnings begin low for young labor force participants and then increase with age until they peak prior to retirement age. This hypothesis predicts periods of dissavings for both the young and the old, with savings during the typically high-income middle years of life. To the extent that the poverty population is in either low-income state, young or old, its members would consume more than their current income by either borrowing against future earnings or drawing down previously accumulated earnings in the form of savings. As such a high proportion of the poor are young, this proposal may explain some of the disparity between expenditures and cash income.

Other possible explanations include (a) overall increases in the amount of debt carried by families; (b) underreporting of annual income; (c) overreporting of annual expenditures; and (d) excluding government in-kind transfers such as housing vouchers, food stamps, and medical care—all of which act to increase purchasing power.

The level of underreporting of income is difficult to quantify, but the size of the underground or informal economy is substantial. For example, the IRS estimated that unreported legal-source income for individuals was $270 billion in 1988 (Internal Revenue Service, 1988), and in 1985 the informal market for a wide range of goods or services (e.g., home repairs, domestic service, lessons, appliance repairs, laundry, and clothing) was about 14.6% of total sales (McCrohan, Smith, & Adams, 1991). This sector of economic activity includes both earnings from illegal activities as well as unreported earnings from legal activities. As much of this income is subject to taxation but is not reported to the Internal Revenue Service, recipients are not likely to report it to other government agencies conducting surveys. Although poor people may be likely to be vendors in the informal economy, they actually spend less money with informal suppliers than do more affluent consumers (McCrohan & Sugrue, 1995).

In short, there is a variety of reasons why annual cash incomes are not consistent with annual purchasing power. Consequently, income criteria for the official poverty rates may understate the ability of the poor to purchase goods and services. This observation is important to marketers when estimating the profitability of entering a low-income market. Clearly, it makes that market more attractive than it would be if the business relied solely on market data that report cash income. Marketers underestimate the financial resources of the poor, both as individuals and in the aggregate. As individuals, their disposable income cannot be judged merely on the basis of cash income; what they have to exchange is greater than that. Thus, poor consumers should not be ignored by businesses. Furthermore, although their financial resources are meager, poor people in urban areas tend to be highly concentrated, so as an aggregate market they can be a profitable market segment.

SUMMARY AND IMPLICATIONS

For academics and public policymakers, there is a challenge to assess the effects of the current poverty threshold on the uses of alternative financial resources and to find alternative ways to define the poverty threshold that both identify needs and take the various financial resources into account. For public policymakers and social service providers, supportive "safety net" programs should be separated from "bootstrap" programs. The uses of these two types of programs depend on a good estimate of financial resources of the recipients of the programs.

The amount of time spent by a person in poverty as a way to segment poor consumers also has implications for marketers, academics, public policymakers, and social service providers. For marketers, those temporarily in poverty are more likely to have more discretionary financial resources in the near future and so the relationship with them as customers should be nurtured. The resources of those who are poor for a longer period of time are limited and will continue to be limited for a period of time, so their resources must be carefully used. For example, they need goods that offer value and are not priced to subsidize unnecessary and unwanted added value.

For public policymakers and social service providers, people likely to be in poverty for different amounts of time should be identified and supported with different programs. Those expected to be in poverty for a short time require short-term programs and incentive and other help in exiting poverty. For example, they need safety net programs to ensure that the basic needs of food, housing, and transportation are satisfied. Those expected to be poor for a longer time require other incentives. There is a need for academics to examine the differential needs of these segments of the poor as well as appropriate incentives and programs to address their different needs.

BEHAVIORAL CHARACTERISTICS
OF THE POOR CONSUMER

Social scientists who considered poverty in the 1960s and 1970s characterized the behavior of poor people as different from their more affluent counterparts (e.g., Martineau, 1958; see review by Berkman & Gilson, 1976). For example, people in the "lower-lower" class were described as "marked by with despair, anger, and apathy" (Berkman & Gilson, 1976, p. 648). Martineau (1958) hypothesized that poor people differ in some key cognitive characteristics. He suggested that poor people focus more on the present and past than on the future. Consequently, they use a shorter time frame and, as a result, are less inclined to delay gratification. He also suggested that poor people tend to be concrete thinkers rather than abstract thinkers and are "essentially nonrational" in their thinking. He further suggested they are limited in the processes they use to make choices. These imputed characteristics are consistent with the argument by several social scientists in the 1970s that a "culture of poverty" exists—that is, the poverty population shares not only low income but norms, values, and aspirations that differ from those of the balance of society.

Although the poor may share certain common ways of behaving, it is not clear whether these common characteristics are due to their personal inclinations or propensities or to the situation in which they find themselves. Before one can attribute observed behavioral differences of the poor to a culture of poverty, one must consider the limited opportunities that the poor face relative to the rest of society. Schiller (1995), for example, argues that before one can attribute behavioral differences between less and more affluent people to a culture of poverty, several conditions must be met. First, both poor and nonpoor must face the same potential benefits in deferring satisfaction from obtaining goods and services. Second, both the poor and the nonpoor must equally suffer from the deferment. Third, the probability of obtaining gratification after deferment must be equal for the poor and the nonpoor. If in reality low income and limited opportunities of the poor yield incentives different from those operating for the balance of the population, the observed behavioral differences are not attributable to differences in culture. Consider two consumer behavior processes—how people perceive time and how much control people believe they have over their own fate.

PERCEPTION OF TIME

Time may be perceived differently by people from different social classes. Graham (1981) suggests that upper classes use *linear time* whereas low social classes use nonlinear time. People who use linear time, the common basis for Western time perception, consider time as a commodity to be divided up, measured, and allocated to different tasks. People who use *procedural time* organize time in terms of the tasks to be accomplished. For example, for people on procedural time, a meeting starts "when the time is right," but for people on linear time, a meeting starts at 2 p.m. Procedural time tends to focus more on the present whereas linear time focuses more on the future. Consistent with the tendency for the poor to use procedural time, Oscar Lewis (1969) reports that the poor generally have a time orientation in the present. Luria (1976) reports more concrete rather than abstract thinking among poor and powerless people, which is consistent with a time perception system focused on the present. In a qualitative study of street groups of young African American men in the inner city in the 1960s, Horton (1967) reports that, for these men, time perception depends on what is happening in terms of the people who are present and opportunities to get money (such as "hustling"). Time depends on events and is procedural rather than linear: "Time is alive when and where there is action" (p. 8). Horton explained this time perspective by suggesting that because the lives of these young Black men were less under their own control than were lives of the more affluent members of society, linear, or clock, time was not especially relevant. Rather, chance events such as meeting someone to "hang out with" or "hustling"—finding a place to make money—offered more relevant opportunities. If poor people do use procedural time and are more focused on the present than the future, then one implication is that they will not be inclined to plan for the future. For example, they will not consider the benefits of an education that does not pay off until the future. They will not consider the financial benefits of saving for an appliance rather than buying it on time at a high rate of interest.

   Other research contradicts these claims. In a review of personality correlates of poverty, Allen (1970) reports that empirical evidence does not support the idea that the poor have a shorter time perspective or are less inclined to delay gratification. Similarly, a more contemporary empirical study of Martineau's (1958) proposals (Hendon, Williams, & Huffman, 1988) also does not support the idea that poor people use a shorter time frame in thinking about the effects of events. Furthermore, there is little relation between social class and whether credit cards are used for convenience or for revolving debt (Dominquez & Page, 1981). In any event, poor consumers generally have little opportunity to obtain credit cards.

There is a way to reconcile these seemingly conflicting results. Perceiving and using time as a way to mark events (procedural time) rather than as a commodity (linear time) would seem to be an appropriate reaction of poor people to their situation. It is highly adaptive to take advantage of opportunities and events that enhance one's economic or social life. If this means responding to events as they occur, it may be perceived as focusing on the present and, in general, using procedural time. When the future is uncertain, thinking in terms of the future makes little sense. The adage used by Alcoholics Anonymous to help their members through their stressful lives might also be an adaptive guide for people under stress from poverty: one day at a time. People who live in poverty may be quite capable of using linear time when it is called for, however, such as when asked to rate statements about time perception on a questionnaire. "The problem is not a deficient sense of time but deficient knowledge and control to make a fantasy future and a really better life possible" (Horton, 1967, p. 8).

For people who are net consumers and only have enough resources to satisfy their short-term needs, it is not only logical but adaptive to take a short-term perspective. On the other hand, people cannot survive without plans, hopes, and dreams (Miller, Galanter, & Pribram, 1960). To the extent that consumer products fulfill these dreams (e.g., McCracken, 1981), poor consumers as well as more affluent ones are enculturated by products.

If poor consumers do actually use a short time frame, or even if they are perceived to do so, they are likely to be treated differently by marketers. Marketers are less likely to trust that people who use a short time frame will fulfill contracts that last over time like paying for products over time. They also are less likely to consider building a customer relationship that will last over more than a single transaction.

Public policymakers and social service providers may see this characteristic as one that is subject to training. But because a short time frame may be due to the situation of having few financial resources rather than to individual ability or propensity, it may be inappropriate to direct training efforts to this topic. An implication for academics is that they should devote research to those aspects of a culture of poverty that can and should be changed to make a consumer less vulnerable or more effective.

HELPLESSNESS AND LOCUS OF CONTROL

In the 1960s and 1970s, the poor were reported to perceive themselves as relatively deprived, manipulated externally, powerless, and alienated (Andreasen, 1975). Consistent with this, the poor have been characterized as believing they have little control over their own fate; that is, their lives are controlled more by external events (external locus of control) than by acts they initiate (internal locus of control) (Rotter, 1966). Indeed, poor people, particularly single mothers, are less confident, less willing to take risks, and more likely to believe their lives are controlled by external events (Salling & Harvey, 1981). One study (Eckenrode, 1983) found that as income increased for low-income women who believe they do have control over their own lives (high internal locus of control), they made more use of support people to help them in times of stress. Poor women who believe they control their own fate are more likely to seek out help from others but only if they also have more than a minimal amount of financial resources.

It is realistic for poor people to believe they are powerless. In fact, women are more likely to believe their lives are driven by external events (high external locus of control) when they are the single head of families in which they actually do have little control over their income. Their income is controlled by others, as it comes from AFDC payments, public assistance, or alimony (Bould, 1977). For a person who observes that he or she has a limited opportunity to make choices, as poor people do (Horton, 1967), it is only realistic to believe that life is controlled by events not under personal influence. As an example, consider the experience of a participant-observer who served as a blood donor in a lower-income neighborhood (Kretzmann, 1992). He described how poor people were demeaned by the staff of the blood donor center. The staff demanded passivity and compliance from donors, and there was a lot of time spent waiting, as though the clients' time was of little value.

In sum, poor people do tend to attribute control of their behavior to external forces and believe they have little control over their own fate. This is not an unrealistic point of view. As we propose in Chapter 9, one way to more equally balance marketing exchanges that involve poor consumers is to increase their power in the exchange. By doing this, poor consumers may be more likely to perceive that they do indeed control their own lives.

REACTANCE

Another characteristic related to feeling powerless is *reactance*. Reactance means you are less attracted to behaviors or attitudes that are forced on you. It is experienced when a consumer's expected freedom of choice is threatened (Clee & Wicklund, 1980). For poor people, reactance may be expressed by their rejection of certain values of the more affluent population. For instance, some inner-city African American youth reject the values associated with education.

Whether reactance will be experienced or not may depend on a consumer's reference group; a person may only feel deprived of choices if other people who are relevant to that person, that person's reference group, possess more freedom of choice. If poor people consider their point of reference to be people in their neighborhood, they are less likely to express reactance. If poor people use as a point of reference the people they see on television, reactance is more likely to be experienced. As we will see in Chapter 7, television viewing takes up a good deal of the time of poor people. Hendon et al. (1988) found that lower-class respondents do feel restricted in their freedom of choice. One might expect that this feeling might translate to reactance in the consumer domain for poor people. For example, they might adopt a different fashion in hairstyle, clothing, or behavior—as some poor young people do.

SUMMARY AND IMPLICATIONS

Demographic characteristics and the geographic distribution of poor consumers is important targeting information for those who market products and services to them, as well as for regulators and social service providers. It is important for marketers and regulators to be aware that the modal poor consumer is not an inner-city dweller. Poor consumers are demographically diverse and have diverse needs for goods and services.

Because poor consumers' diversity results in different needs, approaches to solving problems in exchanges with marketers should be tailored to different segments within this population. For example, a poor rural consumer has different problems of access to products and services than does a poor urban consumer. Similarly, effective marketing communication media and messages would be different for poor disabled consumers than for poor single moms. The high incidence of children in poverty suggests that either the marketplace should respond to needs of families with children by producing low-cost, "no-frills," family-size packages of products consumed by this type of family or regulators should provide incentives to encourage the distribution of products for this segment. The lower level of educational attainment by people in poverty implies that marketing information should be tailored to their capabilities. The use of clear language, many graphics, and unambiguous information would benefit both the consumer and the marketer.

The actual income levels reported by poor consumers, a figure often referred to by marketers in obtaining consumption information from marketing services, can be a misleading indicator of the purchasing power of these consumers. Marketers may find that poor consumers can, in fact, purchase more than their cash incomes may indicate—that is, they are a more profitable segment than their cash income suggests. This may be attributed to a variety of reasons, but it is in large part due to the volatility of the poverty population. A significant number of the poor are poor for short periods of time and are able to either consume previous savings or draw down future earnings—they are not long-term poor consumers.

Finally, although poor consumers may exhibit behavioral characteristics different from those of more affluent consumers, these characteristics may be due to their situation rather than to their individual abilities and personalities. As the economic situation improves for poor people, so might their behavior. The behavioral characteristics discussed in this chapter have implications for the behavior of poor consumers in the marketplace. First, their tendency to feel they have little control over their own fate suggests that poor consumers might be easily manipulated by marketers and need protection by education or regulation. It also suggests that they are less likely than more affluent consumers to complain when they are unfairly, illegally, or inappropriately treated in the marketplace. Second, the possibility that poor consumers exhibit reactance, being less attracted to behaviors forced on them, is likely to be enhanced by the limited products, services, and retail outlets available to them. This suggests that products available in their usual outlets may be perceived to be less attractive than products in less frequently used outlets. Thus, even if the quality and variety of products is brought to a parity with more affluent neighborhoods, poor consumers may resist recognizing that parity.

NOTES

1. Copyright © 1995 by the Chicago Tribune Company. All rights reserved. Used with permission.

2. The data in Table 4.1 begin in 1973 because it is the first year that the U.S. Bureau of the Census began providing annual poverty rates for Hispanics. The U.S. Bureau of the Census classifies Hispanics as an ethnic group rather than a race, as both Whites and African Americans may be Hispanic. Poverty rates are available for Whites and children beginning in 1959 but do not become available for African Americans until 1966 and for the elderly until 1967. All of these series mimic the aggregate trend between 1959 and 1972.

3. These numbers do not sum to 100% because the groups are not mutually exclusive. Both Whites and African Americans may be Hispanic.

4. According to the *Statistical Abstract of the United States* (1994, Table 100), the percentage of all live births accounted for by unwed mothers was 11% in 1970 and 30% in 1991. For Whites, the percentages are 6% and 22%, respectively; for African Americans, the rates are 38% and 68%, respectively.

5. This rate is even higher for African American and Hispanic children. In 1992, they faced poverty rates of 46.6% and 39.9%, respectively.

6. About 21% of the working-age poor who are not working give other reasons than those mentioned for not working. If we accept illness, lack of jobs, and caretaker requirements as valid reasons for not working, this implies that only 10.8% of the working-age poor do not work when we would expect them to do so. Approximately 90% of the working-age poor we would expect to work do so.

7. To the extent that the decrease in earnings is due to the performance of the economy rather than voluntary reductions in hours worked, independent of prevailing wages, these decreases in earnings are attributed to macroeconomic conditions.

8. Some of this family dissolution may be due to economic conditions—to the extent that changes in national or local economic conditions lead to decreases in family income, they may exacerbate tensions within families and possibly increase the rate of family dissolution. Consequently, the estimates of poverty starts caused by demographic characteristics should be taken as an upper-bound estimate of the noneconomic effects.

9. These calculations are by the authors based on Consumer Expenditure Survey (CEX) interview data. The unit of analysis is neither individuals nor families but consumer units. Thus, the estimates are not strictly comparable to official poverty rates based on Current Population Survey (CPS) data and are somewhat higher than those from CPS data (15.1%).

5

Consumption of Products
and Services by the Poor

How different are poor consumers from more affluent ones in buying products they need for everyday living? Do poor consumers, many of whom receive public assistance for their consumption of food and shelter, "abuse" assistance by spending money on luxuries? Are they "wise" consumers in that they choose food products that provide nutrition and contribute to good health? What barriers do poor consumers face when they look for a place to live? Do poor consumers use more "sin" products such as tobacco and alcohol than the average consumer?

A welfare mother, talking about shopping for her five-year-old son and herself: "Dan and I buy clothes at resale shops—nothing new and I buy almost nothing." (Polakow, 1993, p. 4)

The children love Doritos, but at $2.89 a bag at the Save-a-Lot discount store, where Linda Snider buys most of her groceries, they are too expensive. Instead, she buys two bags of generic potato chips for 89 cents, Kool-Aid instead of soda, pork chops instead of steak. Once a month she splurges on a half-gallon of ice cream. "I buy a lot of macaroni and cheese for 19 cents a box," said Mrs. Snider. (Janofsky, 1995, p. A1)[1]

Anthony Gibbons, a homeless man with poor teeth, says he often goes hungry between welfare checks but, when he can, faithfully buys three cans of Nutrament a day. "It's an athlete's drink," says the soft-spoken former crack addict. . . . Nutrament, which flopped as a power drink for athletes more than a decade ago, has been born again and repackaged as a meal-in-a-can for inner-city residents, among them the poor, addicted and the homeless. . . . While $2 may be pricey for a drink, it is cheap for dinner. (Hwang, 1994, p. A1)[2]

In this chapter, we look at how the poor cope with satisfying basic needs such as food, housing, and transportation. We also look at the marketing of sin products, such as alcohol and tobacco, and how they are consumed by poor people.

WHAT DO POOR PEOPLE SPEND ON BASIC NEEDS?

Although overall expenditures are obviously lower for low-income households, poor people consume many of the same products and services as the rest of the population. All households, including those with low incomes, spend the most on housing, food, and transportation. Poor consumers differ in being " 'net consumers,' spending nearly all of their monthly income to secure the basics" (Consumers Union, 1993, p. 14). As the above quotations illustrate, there is little room for discretionary spending.

In low-income households, more than two thirds of the budget is spent on nondiscretionary items (Ambry, 1993). Low-income women whose marriages have been dissolved spend about half of their budget on housing and food alone; the rest must cover transportation, clothing, and everything else (Weiss, 1984).

When expenditures by low-income households are compared to average households for different categories of products, two key points stand out. First, the percentages of expenditures on food and housing by poor households are greater than for the average household. Second, the poor spend a much smaller percentage on items that provide a financial cushion for emergencies, such as insurance, pensions, and social security. Table 5.1

TABLE 5.1 Average Annual Expenditures for Products and Services by Low-Income Versus All Households

	All Consumer Units		Income Under $10,000	
Food	$4,367	14%	$2,323	16%
Alcohol and tobacco	592	2	309	2
Housing	11,494	37	6,248	44
Apparel and services	2,220	7	1,003	7
Transportation	5,235	17	1,788	13
Health care	1,563	5	1,032	7
Entertainment	1,523	5	587	4
Insurance	354	1	103	1
Pensions/Social security	2,788	9	185	1
Education and reading	602	2	423	3
Other	671	2	251	2
Total expenditures	$31,409	100%	$14,252	100%

SOURCE: Ambry (1993, pp. 352-353); data from U.S. Department of Labor, Survey of Labor Statistics (1992).

shows expenditures for different categories of products by low- and average-income households.

DO THE POOR GET ENOUGH TO EAT?

"I've given up on this child—she's socially dysfunctional—three times now we've caught her stealing free lunch and storing it in her desk to take home!" . . . The child of a single mother, she lived with her sister and mother in a trailer park. They all appeared chronically hungry, particularly when food stamps ran out before the end of the month. Apparently, Heather had been caught stealing extra free lunch on three Fridays, knowing that she and her sister would have to wait until Monday for their next free meals. (Polakow, 1993, p. 2)

Although the poorest Americans spend a larger percentage of their resources on food, some do not eat as well as the rest of us.

- A recent U.S. government-sponsored report indicates that about 30 million Americans who are poor fail to eat enough food ("30 Million Hungry," 1992).
- About 16% of people aged 60 or more are malnourished because they are too poor or too incapacitated to obtain and prepare meals (McCarthy, 1994).

- A 1977 USDA Food Consumption Survey indicated that 13.4% of low-income households report they sometimes or often did not get enough to eat, and 53.7% report the amount of food was barely adequate (Blaylock, 1991).

DO POOR PEOPLE SPEND
THEIR FOOD DOLLARS WISELY?

When you are severely limited in how much you can spend for food, you may be able to buy enough food, but the food you buy may not be satisfying or appropriate. People who can only afford "filling foods" like rice and bread may well bemoan the lack of variety in their diets and consider them inadequate. On the other hand, it is possible that poor people may compensate for their inability to purchase other more expensive products by spending relatively more money than the average household on easily accessible "gratification" foods such as sweets. They may try to reduce the high levels of stress under which they live by reducing their food preparation efforts and buying convenience foods.

It is possible that as a way to compensate for their inability to purchase other more expensive products, poor people may consume less healthy or more expensive kinds of foods. For example, a 1990 Nielsen study reported that low-income households purchased certain products more than did other households: frozen pizza, pork rinds, beef patties, and corn dogs ("Shops in Inner Cities," 1992). Spending inappropriately on food might mean eating out of the home rather than less expensively at home, eating more gratification foods, buying more prepared or convenience foods, and preparing more satisfying but less healthy foods.

To examine this idea, we analyzed data from the 1991 Consumer Expenditure Survey sponsored by the U.S. Department of Labor. The amount spent on selected food items by low-income households (income less than $10,000 a year) was compared to the amount spent by average households.[3] An index was computed to control for both the amount spent by the average household for that particular food item and the amount spent for food consumed at home by households with annual incomes under $10,000.[4] In general, poor households made appropriate choices of foods given their financial constraints. First, poor people were much less likely to eat out. The amount they spent for food consumed at home was 19% higher by households with incomes under $10,000 than for all households. The amount poor households spent for food consumed away from home was 31% lower than for all households.

TABLE 5.2 Index of Ratio for Selected Food Product Share of In-Home Food Expenditures for Households With Incomes Under $10,000 Versus All Households

Food Expenditure	Index
Filling foods	112
Rice	109
Pasta, other cereals	110
Bread	114
Gratification foods	86
Cookies/crackers	87
Candy	96
Chips, nuts, snacks	78
Ingredient foods	118
Flour	177
Eggs	130
Sugar	134
Butter	105
Convenience foods	92
Prepared canned/packaged foods	93
Frozen prepared foods	93
Flour mixes	87
Frozen bakery products	82
"Unhealthy" foods	105
Red meats (beef, pork, lamb, frankfurters)	112
Fats and oils	105
Snacks	86
"Healthy" foods	101
White meats (chicken and fish)	103
Fresh fruit	96
Fresh vegetables	105
Processed fruit	94
Processed vegetables	109

SOURCE: U.S. Department of Labor, Survey of Labor Statistics (1992).

Second, poor households spent food dollars wisely. Table 5.2 reports indexes for selected food items categorized into four types: convenience foods, gratification foods, filling foods, and ingredient foods. An index of 100 represents parity with the average household. Poor households spent 14% less on prepared gratification foods or snacks than the average household (index = 86). They spent less on convenience foods like prepared canned or frozen foods and mixes (index = 92). In contrast, they spent 18% more money on ingredient items such as flour, eggs, milk, butter, and sugar. The average, low-income household spent about 12% more on filling foods like rice, pasta, and bread than all households combined (index = 112). Low-income households appeared to spend about the same as all households for healthy (index = 101) and for unhealthy (index = 105) foods. In sum, poor households use their resources prudently by preparing foods from scratch and avoiding convenience foods. They find ways to stretch the food budget with filling foods and avoid expensive snack foods.

PUBLIC PERCEPTIONS OF WHAT THE POOR EAT

Public attitudes about welfare and poverty may be influenced by what the public *believes* poor people eat. This is likely to be particularly true for the nonpoor public. For example, if the public believes poor people spend their money unwisely on food, this belief can bolster a negative attitude to the poor and to welfare programs. Public attitudes about welfare and poverty, in turn, influence the legislators and regulators who make public policy. If public perceptions about what poor people eat are incorrect, they can result in inappropriate public policy actions.

To explore public perceptions of how poor households spend their food dollars, we surveyed a sample of the nonpoor public (Alwitt, 1995). Perceptions of food expenditures by the poor were elicited from a survey of 300 Midwestern nonpoor people. The sample consisted of 135 students, younger respondents who represent attitudes of future voters; 140 persons intercepted in a shopping mall, older respondents who represent attitudes of current voters; and 25 persons who work for social service agencies or have other professional concern with the poor and represent experts who are thought to have a greater than average influence on public policymakers. Differences in perceptions by these three subsamples can provide insights about how the public influences policymakers. Note that this is a convenience sample that is geographically limited and must be considered an exploratory survey.

Survey respondents were asked to judge whether the proportion of income spent by poor households for each of eight foods was much less, somewhat less, the same, much more, or somewhat more than that spent by the average-income household. The foods included in the survey can be categorized as healthy foods (poultry, rice, pasta, and bread) and unhealthy foods (snacks, frankfurters, and red meats). As a whole, the

TABLE 5.3 Perceptions of Amounts Spent for Selected Foods by Poor Households Compared to Average Households

			Group		
Food	Total	Younger	Older	Experts	F-ratio
Unhealthy foods					
Snacks	3.20	3.30	4.13	2.92	10.49[*]
Beef	2.21	2.07	2.83	2.23	5.88[*]
Pork	2.50	2.59	3.17	2.29	7.31[*]
Frankfurters	3.10	3.89	4.04	3.57	4.40[**]
Healthy foods					
Poultry	3.75	2.96	3.52	3.09	n.s.
Rice	3.60	3.62	3.52	3.67	n.s.
Pasta	3.39	3.28	3.17	3.52	n.s.
Bread	3.77	3.82	3.61	3.79	n.s.

NOTE: The rating scale is: 1 = much less; 2 = somewhat less; 3 = same; 4 = somewhat more; 5 = much more.
$*p < .005$; $**p < .01$; n.s. = not significant.

respondents believed that poor households spend relatively more for snacks, franks, rice, pasta, and bread; relatively less for beef and pork; and the same for poultry (confirmed by z-tests that compare mean ratings with the middle rating). Table 5.3 reports the mean judgments of expenditures for each food by the total sample as well as by each of the three subsamples.

Some of these perceptions of what the poor eat are inaccurate compared to the actual consumption of these foods by poor households. Using data from the Consumer Expenditure Survey for 1991, we controlled for the amount spent on food at home. Compared to the average, poor households spend relatively *less* on snacks, more on frankfurters and pork, and about the same for beef. Poor households spend more on pasta and bread and about as much on poultry and rice. In other words, the respondents had inaccurate perceptions of what poor consumers spend on four of these eight food items.

A comparison of the three subsamples, however, does show differences in perceptions of the amount spent for healthy and unhealthy foods by poor consumers. Compared to the other groups, the older respondents believed poor people spent *more* on the four unhealthy foods. In contrast, the experts believed that poor consumers spent *less* than average on snacks, pork, and frankfurters. To the extent that perceptions of what poor people eat influence attitudes about welfare and poverty, older people are more likely to have negative attitudes and experts are more likely to have positive attitudes. For none of the surveyed groups is there a significant correlation between the perceived and actual amounts spent by poor consumers (relative to the average) for the eight food items. In other words, neither the general nonpoor public nor the experts accurately perceive how much poor consumers spend on each of these food items.

To the extent that one can draw general conclusions from this survey, none of the subsamples, younger people (future voters), older people (current voters), or experts (influencers), have an accurate idea of what poor people spend on this list of foods. These unrealistic perceptions negatively bias most people's attitudes about poverty and welfare and can inappropriately influence public policymakers.

FOOD ASSISTANCE PROGRAMS

If the poor do not eat enough or the right kinds of foods, what resources are available to them? Several government and private food assistance programs exist to ensure that poor consumers in this nation do not starve. Food assistance programs not only help the poor but also benefit food businesses. They increase sales of products for a population that would otherwise buy less.

The best-known governmental food assistance program is the food stamp program. As noted in Chapter 3, benefit levels vary by state and family size; the Bureau of Labor Statistics estimated an average monthly benefit of $150 per poor household in 1990. Not all eligible families participate in the food stamp program. DeParle (1993) estimated that only about 60% of those eligible actually participated in 1992. Nevertheless, in the early 1990s, there were a record number of food stamp recipients (DeParle, 1993). Food stamps do appear to provide a needed service: Compared to participants in the food stamp program, nonparticipants suffer from nutritional deficiencies (Bishop, Formby, & Zeager, 1992).

Food stamp programs are not perfect. Recipients of food stamps often are hard pressed to obtain sufficient sustenance and often run out before the end of the month. Food stamp fraud is perpetrated by some recipients and merchants. In an effort to reduce fraud (e.g., Raab, 1993), several states are experimenting with the use of electronic food stamps. Other experiments include the use of food stamps for items other than food, at the discretion of the recipient ("Debate Stirs," 1994).[5]

Another governmental food assistance program is WIC, the Special Supplemental Food Program for Women, Infants, and Children. This program provides vouchers for groceries, often specifying the brands that can be purchased. Eligible participants are pregnant and nursing women and their children under 5 years of age. This program benefits a large number of needy (the program had about 4.5 million participants in 1992); it also benefits food manufacturers because sales can be substantial. For this reason, firms make efforts to ensure their brands are included on the WIC list. For example, firms that manufacture infant formulas engage in political lobbying or offer rebates to the states for cans of formula purchased by a WIC participant. A further advantage to brands approved for WIC purchases is based on a classic marketing adage: A brand with which a consumer is familiar is likely to be preferred over an unfamiliar brand (Gibson, 1993).

Although food assistance programs offer the obvious benefit to poor consumers of allowing them to purchase needed food they might not otherwise be able to afford, they also have less-positive effects on low-income consumers. Some nonrecipients of these programs are hostile to recipients:

> "My oldest daughter, she graduated from middle school. And she told me last year that she did not want to receive the hot lunch program because the children made a difference. So I had to scrape for the last couple of years while she was in middle school and try to make ends meet so that I could send her with a dollar or two dollars every day. Which is a big chunk out of our budget." (Rank, 1994, p. 139)

Users of food stamps also report being treated more negatively in food stores (Rank, 1994). Because of this anticipated negative experience, poor people are less likely to shop at stores outside their immediate neighborhood (Polakow, 1993) even though they could save money and choose from a larger variety of products and brands at those stores.

Private sources of food for poor people are charitable food pantries, soup kitchens, and food banks. The largest network of food banks is Second Harvest, which has almost 200 member centers and supplies about 46,000 local agencies (Ingram, 1993). Charitable soup kitchens and food pantries receive cash donations and products from hunger marches and

food drives and contributions from individuals, businesses, and government and religious institutions (Romano, 1992). Food corporations and
grocery chains donate money to food banks as well as unsalable products,
such as those with damaged packaging.

Poor people also receive food from government food programs such as
the Emergency Food Assistance Program (TEFAP) and the Federal Emergency Management Agency (FEMA). FEMA provides basic items such as
tuna and pasta ("TEFAP and FEMA," 1994). TEFAP is a key source of
basic foods such as butter, flour, and canned vegetables. But the program,
which is intended for people with incomes less than 125% of the poverty
level, served fewer people in recent years due to a decrease in the amount
of surplus food.

Food banks are subject to changes in the food industry and society and in
recent years have seen donations fall. They cannot rely on monetary and
governmental donations as much as in the past (Ingram, 1993, 1994; Lewin,
1994). Because of increased efficiencies in manufacturing and marketing,
food manufacturers also have provided less food. As a result of the decrease
in food and monetary resources from both private and governmental sources,
some food banks have resorted to self-production by, for example, developing
a food-dehydrating plant to produce food for the needy (Lewin, 1994).

SUMMARY AND IMPLICATIONS

In summary, the poor may not receive enough food or the right kinds
of foods, and their access to food seems to be becoming more limited.
Because there is some evidence that the nonpoor public does not know
how poor consumers spend their food dollars, there is a need to provide
accurate information to the public at large and to public policymakers on
at least two issues: (a) what and how much poor people eat and (b) the
appropriate role of food assistance in the welfare system.

Food assistance programs are quite distinct from other welfare programs. They serve as a safety net rather than as a bootstrap program.
Although food assistance provides a safety net, it is not designed to help
poor people *escape* poverty. Nevertheless, expenditures on food assistance
programs are inappropriately tracked as indicators of the success of
governmental spending to decrease the poverty level (Northrop, 1991).
The creation and implementation of food assistance programs should not
depend on whether a poor person is perceived as worthy but rather on the

obligation of a society to ensure minimal subsistence standards for its members.

Marketers and manufacturers of food products are faced with conflicts with regard to poor consumers. Generally, marketers do not consider poor consumers as a unique segment of the target market. Segmentation is more likely to be based on frequency and quantity of purchase, food preparation styles, or other criteria that are only indirectly related to income. But the use of accepted marketing practices places poor consumers at a disadvantage. For example, competitive pressures encourage marketers to introduce variations on a basic product (such as chocolate chip cookies with peanut butter, with pecans, with chunky chips, or with a soft texture). These variations on the basic product increase the costs of manufacturing, packaging, advertising, and trade and consumer promotions, and the increased costs are likely to be passed on to the consumer. Although food businesses may believe that product variety strengthens their competitive positions, the increased price limits the products that poor consumers can afford to buy.

Food businesses also face another ethical conflict. Several food businesses have been most generous in donating certain products to food banks. Competitive pressures and demands for financial responsibility have resulted in, among other corporate changes, increased operational efficiencies. This is, of course, a healthy and appropriate action by the food corporation, but it also results in less food available for donation to food banks. Given that its prime objective is to run a successful business, how much of an obligation does a food producer have to needy segments of society? When one of its channels to these segments is reduced or eliminated, how much are businesses morally obligated to open another channel for charitable purposes?

PLACES TO LIVE

Housing constitutes 34% of expenditures for families in poverty and is their largest single expenditure (computed from the 1989 Consumer Expenditure Survey). The most common forms of housing for poor people are private rentals, public housing, and single room occupancy (SRO) hotels.

Poor consumers are more likely to rent than to own homes. In 1991, expenditures for renting a home were 117% greater for poor households (incomes of $10,000 or less) but 22% lower for owning a home (Ambry, 1993). Traditionally, a sign of financial security is paying 30% or less of one's income for rent, which is about the average paid in the United States (Ambry, 1993). In 1987, 21% of the 32.7 million renter households paid more than 50% of their income for rental housing, and 12.3% paid more than 70% of their income for rent (Braus, 1991).

Poor people generally live in older housing, which is less well insulated against weather and often in need of repairs. It is not surprising, then, that poor consumers pay more for utilities and home maintenance. Relative to all households (and controlling for their total level of expenditures), households with incomes less than $10,000 pay 35% more to maintain their homes and 51% more for utilities (computed from Consumer Expenditure Survey; Ambry, 1993).

OWNING A HOME

A central component of the American dream is owning a home. It is a financially sound investment for the owner, and the community benefits because resident homeowners have a greater commitment to the community.

Low-income consumers who want to own their dwellings often have more difficulty than more affluent households in financing this investment. This is particularly true for members of minority groups (Thomas, 1992). Mortgage lenders are required by the federal Community Investment Act to get input from the community in which they are located and support community needs (Hixon, 1991), but they naturally try to reduce their risks.

Borrowing money to buy a home is a bigger problem for poor consumers than for the rest of society. An analysis in the Boston area indicated that only 20% of loan applicants are clearly qualified or unqualified. The other 80% fall into the gray area in which subjective judgment plays a much greater role (Consumers Union, 1993, p. 70) and low-income consumers are at a disadvantage.

BARRIERS TO BORROWING

There are a number of barriers for low-income consumers in taking out a mortgage loan. If the down payment is large (20% or more), the lender is more likely to overlook negative credit indicators, on the theory that a person with an investment in the property is more likely to keep up the mortgage payments. But many low-income households cannot make large down payments so they do not benefit from this judgment.

Asking for a small loan does not work in favor of a minority or low-income borrower. The lender finds the effort is equal but the profit is lower in making a small versus a large loan and therefore is biased against making small loans. Low-income borrowers also may have income that is not easy to verify, such as from multiple jobs or rent from boarders. Because these borrowers are atypical, lenders are not willing to take the risk of making a loan. In addition, low-income households that do not have a relationship with a bank use currency exchanges and lenders look askance at this way of dealing with money.

Federal Housing Authority (FHA) loans have flexible down payments and are government insured. For example, the debt ratio for most banks is 28:36 (housing debt should be no more than 28% of gross monthly income, and all debts no more than 36% of gross income), but the FHA ratio is 35:55 (Consumers Union, 1993, p. 70). But such loans involve so much paperwork that lenders tend to avoid them (Thomas, 1992).

Finally, the most frequent reason for denial of a mortgage loan is credit history (Stangenes, 1993a). Unpaid debts are more common in low-income households, and even when debts are paid, it is not uncommon for them to be incorrectly recorded on credit records, which creates yet another mark against the borrower.

SUMMARY AND IMPLICATIONS

Low-cost housing is in short supply (Harvey, 1987), and with redevelopment of urban areas, the number of SRO hotels has also decreased (Jencks, 1994). Because the interaction of supply to demand determines the cost of housing, the price of low-cost housing is likely to be high. Many low-income householders pay a greater than average share of their financial resources for housing, diminishing the amount left for other necessities. Barriers to owning a house are formidable for poor people and do not seem to have been lowered significantly despite regulatory efforts.

Marketers of housing for low-income households also face ethical conflicts. On the one hand, they perceive the financial risks of nonpayment of rents or mortgage loans, so they charge high rates or erect other barriers to compensate for these risks. On the other hand, this needed resource is provided by some housing suppliers to poor consumers because not all housing suppliers limit their offerings to housing that offers a higher profit margin.

More low-cost housing is needed, and several governmental and private programs address this need. Many of the programs are flawed, however. For example, it has been argued that federal intervention in housing has exacerbated rather than diminished the decline of neighborhoods (Brad-ford & Cincotta, 1992, p. 233; Caine, 1993). It has been reported that after FHA foreclosures the house is often abandoned and left to decay, becomes vandalized, and contributes to the devaluation of the neighbor-hood (Caine, 1993). As another example, fair housing laws have not been aggressively applied to banks. The growth of secondary mortgage markets (FNMA, or Fannie Mae, and FHLMC, or Freddie Mac), which rely on standardized mortgages, exclude those with lower incomes (Bradford & Cincotta, 1992, p. 264).

One approach with some promise is to allow poor people to acquire equity in public housing. Twenty percent of households with incomes below the poverty level live in public housing (*Statistical Abstract of the United States,* 1994, Table 578). The U.S. Department of Housing and Urban Development has been authorized to sell public housing units since 1974, but it was not until 1986 that a demonstration program was initiated. This program authorized the sale of 1,315 units by 17 public housing authorities. In fact, only 320 units were actually sold during the 50-month evaluation period. That so few units were sold was partially due to administrative problems, but it also was due to an inability to attract qualified potential owners. Tenants who did participate had higher in-comes and more stable work and family lives compared to other public housing tenants (Rohe & Stegman, 1992). In sum, this approach to the housing problems of poor people has not yet been optimally designed.

TRANSPORTATION

The average household spends $5,200 annually on transportation, mostly on motor vehicles. For the average household, only 6% is spent on public transportation ("Transportation's Toll," 1993). For poor con-sumers, transportation often presents a challenge.

Low-income consumers are heavy users of public transportation. Peo-ple with annual incomes of $10,000 or less spend 52% more than average on public transportation (Ambry, 1993). Public transportation includes buses, subways, trams, and other intracity mass transit; taxicabs; and intercity buses.

Low-income urban residents are sometimes poorly served by public transportation. When public transportation is eliminated, the poorest residents are the ones most often affected. Examples of actual or proposed discriminatory elimination of public transportation service have been reported recently in Washington, D.C. (Henderson, 1991a, 1991b), Boston (Ackerman, 1989), and Los Angeles (Simon, Riccardi, & Katz, 1994). Routes in low-income neighborhoods are sometimes assigned the most poorly maintained buses (Fehr, 1991). In Los Angeles, low-income riders were charged more for special passes than the transit system charges for regular passes (Zamichow, 1994).

Poor consumers are less likely to own a motor vehicle—in 1992, 21% less likely (Ambry, 1993). They were 29% less likely than average to have a driver's license, although 62% did have one (Mediamark Research, Inc., 1993). They were 44% less likely than average to drive an automobile, although 49% did so, and even less likely to drive a pickup truck (Mediamark Research, Inc., 1993). Poor consumers spend more on gasoline and motor oil (36% and 65% more, respectively) (Ambry, 1993). This can be attributed either to higher usage of their vehicles or to older vehicles.

In sum, transportation is more time consuming, less convenient, and more of a hindrance for poor consumers in going about their business compared to the rest of society. Low-income consumers are limited in their ability to shop outside their neighborhoods not only by constraints on their resources—many cannot afford private transportation and have limited access to public transportation. Although public transportation is primarily the responsibility of government, potential marketers of products and services to low-income consumers also are affected by this limited access: Low-income consumers who might visit retailers or service providers outside their neighborhoods are limited in their ability to do so.

"SIN" PRODUCTS

Certain products can be classified as sin products because although they may have pleasurable effects on the user, they have negative effects on the well-being of the user or society. These products include alcohol and tobacco.[6]

ALCOHOLIC BEVERAGES

It has often been suggested that one of the causes of poverty is abusive use of sin products, and indeed, a subset of poor people do suffer from substance abuse. Poor ·consumers hold the same perceptions as more affluent consumers about the consequences of drinking alcoholic beverages, however. Like more affluent people, they associate alcoholism with birth defects, drunk driving, and rowdy behavior (Klein & Pittman, 1990).

With the exception of malt liquor, alcohol is not consumed disproportionately more by low-income consumers.

- Low-income households report lower consumption of alcoholic beverages than do more affluent households (Adler et al., 1994; Simmons Market Research Bureau, Inc., 1992).
- When total household expenditures are controlled, the amount spent by households with annual incomes under $10,000 for alcoholic beverages is about the same as for all households (index = 95 derived from Consumer Expenditure Survey; Ambry, 1993).
- A survey of older Boston low-income residents found they were less likely to drink alcoholic beverages than were more affluent people (Meyers, Hingson, Mucatel, Heeren, & Goldman, 1985).
- Most studies comparing White to African American drinking indicate that African Americans consume less alcohol and drink less frequently (Hacker, Collins, & Jacobson, 1987).
- Consistent with the usage data, which do not support findings of excessive use of alcohol by poor consumers, a recent study found that overall alcohol consumption actually *rises* during periods of economic *growth*. During economic growth, of course, there are fewer unemployed and fewer people in poverty.

Alcohol does take its toll from populations that are likely to be poor. The social and health effects of alcohol abuse among African Americans are disproportionately high (Hacker et al., 1987). Consumption of alcohol has been reported to be greater than average and cause abuse problems among a subset of Hispanics, Mexican American men, and, for some products, Puerto Rican men. Mexican American men suffer more from cirrhosis, an alcohol-related disease, and die at a younger age from alcohol-related illnesses than White men (Maxwell & Jacobson, 1989). Although there is little evidence that alcohol consumption increases during difficult economic times or that it is greater in areas with low-income populations, when unemployment rates increase there is an increase in the prevalence of liver cirrhosis, which is often due to alcohol consumption (Smith & Hanham, 1985).

MARKETING OF ALCOHOLIC BEVERAGES

Despite the lower usage of alcohol among many poor consumers, marketers have targeted this segment for certain alcoholic beverages. Alcoholic beverage firms have seized a marketing opportunity offered by a segment of potential consumers without adequately considering the consequences for those consumers or for society.

Malt liquor, with a higher alcohol content than beer, is sold widely in inner-city stores (Sims, 1992) and tends to be bought by young Hispanic and African American men ("Malt Liquors," 1992). Malt liquor sales increased by 23% in 1991 over 1990, compared to 4% for all beers (Teinowitz, 1992). Retail stores in inner cities sometimes use business practices that encourage the use of alcoholic beverages such as malt liquors and fortified wines. These stores are open for many hours, and some sell individual paper cups to customers for convenient consumption. Efforts by community groups to discourage these retailer practices as well as distribution in inner-city neighborhoods have had only short-term successes (Sims, 1992).

Producers of alcoholic beverages sold in inner-city stores appear to be aware of the dubious ethical implications of marketing these products. They profit from sales of fortified wine in poor neighborhoods but hide associations with their other products. For example, Gallo makes two fortified wines, Thunderbird and Night Train, but does not label them with the Gallo name.

More billboards advertise sin products in low-income than in other neighborhoods ("Distilling the Truth," 1992; Maxwell & Jacobson, 1989). For example, in 1989, 70% of more than 2,000 billboards in the city of Baltimore advertised alcohol or tobacco products, and three fourths of them were in poor neighborhoods ("Distilling the Truth," 1992). Furthermore, some advertising themes used by alcohol vendors to the Hispanic community are misleading in their appeal to Hispanic cultural values. For example, an advertising campaign for Glenmore Distilleries could be interpreted to imply that one of their brands was approved by the Catholic church: "The Spanish-language ad showed a priest and a monk gazing toward a light shining from above while holding glasses of Felipe II brandy. Translated, the copy read: 'To drink it is not a sin' " (Maxwell & Jacobson, 1989, p. 31). Social activists claim that alcohol manufacturers are among marketers who popularized the Cinco de Mayo celebration in the United States as an event that calls for drinking; it is considered a minor holiday in Mexico (Maxwell & Jacobson, 1989).

CIGARETTES

A sin product that is more likely to be bought by low-income consumers is cigarettes (Adler et al., 1994). In 1990, people with annual incomes of $20,000 or less were 17% more likely to smoke cigarettes (Simmons Market Research Bureau, Inc., 1991). A higher percentage of African American men and young Mexican Americans smoke than White males (Maxwell & Jacobson, 1989). Not surprising, the incidence of lung cancer and other smoking-related diseases among Hispanics has increased relative to Whites, particularly among men (Maxwell & Jacobson, 1989, p. 16).

Both the African American and Hispanic communities, with disproportionately high poverty rates, have been targeted as market segments by tobacco firms. R. J. Reynolds introduced and later withdrew two brands of cigarettes for these segments after consumer pressure. Uptown was targeted at young African Americans, and the Dakota brand was targeted at downscale blue-collar smokers. Cigarette brands with Spanish names like Dorado and Rio are presumably targeted to Hispanic smokers (Maxwell & Jacobson, 1989, p. 37).

The higher incidence of smoking among low-income consumers undoubtedly has influenced the pricing of cigarettes. There is a trend toward increased sales of "discount" cigarettes; in 1992 they had a 30% share of the market compared to zero share in 1981. This trend was one reason the largest tobacco company, Philip Morris, lowered the price of their leading brand, Marlboro. This well-publicized price decrease has been interpreted as an example of "everyday low prices" by leading consumer goods marketers. An alternative explanation is that it targets low-income smokers by appealing to their price sensitivity.

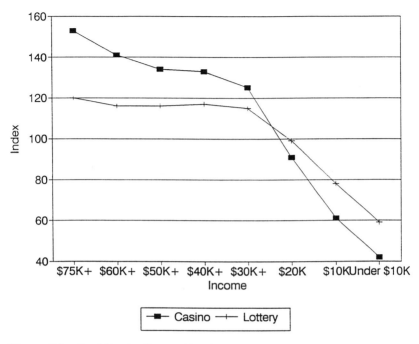

Figure 5.1. Gambling by Income Level
SOURCE: Data from Simmons Market Research Bureau, Inc. (1991).

GAMBLING

Just as we find that poor people do not spend disproportionately more on alcohol, fewer poor people gamble compared to the more affluent. Self-reports in surveys on the incidence of gambling are likely to be biased because the respondent may perceive social disapproval of this activity and fail to report it, but the survey data do show that poor people are less likely to gamble. There is a positive relationship between income and both casino gambling and purchase of lottery tickets. As can be seen in Figure 5.1, people with higher incomes are more likely to purchase lottery tickets and attend gambling casinos (Simmons Market Research Bureau, Inc., 1991). These trends are consistent with those from another survey using a similar methodology (Mediamark Research, Inc., 1993). Also, there is less pari-mutuel horse race betting by people with incomes less than about $12,000 (Thalheimer & Ali, 1992).

Although it appears that fewer poor people gamble, those who do gamble may spend a larger relative proportion of their financial resources doing so. One organization concludes, "State lotteries place greater relative burden on low-income families because low-income groups spend a higher percentage of their income on lottery tickets than do high-income groups" (Selinger, 1993, p. 23). These conclusions are supported by state data about lottery ticket sales. On an aggregate level, state lottery ticket sales increase with state income, with an elasticity of about 3.9. Sales are also sensitive to the state unemployment rate, however, increasing by about 0.17% for each 1% increase in that rate (Mikesell, 1994).

SUMMARY AND IMPLICATIONS

Marketing of sin products in poor neighborhoods demonstrates a conflict of the marketing concept with consideration of the societal good. Firms typically market what consumers demand, but when these products result in health or social problems, marketers face the ethical conflict between following the marketing concept and acting for the good of society by altering their products or withdrawing them from sale.

Alcohol and tobacco firms face other conflicts when they market their brands. For example, positioning alcohol or tobacco by creating associations to the culture of the target market is a standard marketing practice. But when the product has harmful effects for the user or for society, this standard marketing tactic borders on the unethical. One observer of marketing to Hispanics noted in frustration, "They [marketers] know more about our culture than I think health service providers know" (Maxwell & Jacobson, 1989, p. 31).

Finally, corporate contributions by tobacco and alcohol firms to African American or Hispanic conferences and causes are often welcomed, but they also can be considered a means of co-opting community resistance to their products. For example, an agreement between Coors beer and several Hispanic organizations involved an increase in business arrangements with Hispanics as well as large contributions by Coors to the organizations and cessation of a boycott of Coors beer by Hispanics; other members of the Hispanic community objected to the agreement on ethical grounds (Maxwell & Jacobson, 1989).

As this section makes clear, the poor are not heavy users of sin products, but when alcohol and tobacco are abused, the effects are probably more serious than for more affluent people. More important, the use of sin products, such as drinking and gambling, is often perceived as the behavior of a person who is an "unworthy" member of society. The generally lower use of these sin products gives the lie to the stereotype of a poor person as an unworthy member of society.

NOTES

1. Copyright © 1995 by the New York Times Company. Reprinted by permission.

2. Reprinted by permission of the *Wall Street Journal*. Copyright © 1994 by the Dow Jones & Company, Inc. All rights reserved worldwide.

3. The average amount spent for food consumed at home was selected rather than total expenditures on food to control for the higher proportion of income spent on food in general by low-income households (see Table 5.1).

4. Here is an example of how the index is computed: In 1991, all households spent an average of $65.01 for cookies and crackers, whereas the low-income households spent an average of $35.75. The sum of expenditures for food consumed at home was $2,724.89 for all households and $1,722.02 for low-income households. The index for cookies and crackers is:

$$\$35.75 \ / \ ((\$65.01 \times \$1,722.02)/\$2,724.89) = 87.$$

The index of 87 indicates that low-income households spend 13% less on cookies and crackers than expected based on the amount spent by all households and on the amount spent on food consumed at home.

5. The results of these tests suggest that recipients use the stamps less for food and more for transportation and rent, uses that are not to the financial benefit of the food industry.

6. They also include illegal drugs, but data about this underground market are not readily available and are not included in this review.

6

Financial Management and Money-Saving Techniques

Listen honey, if you want to see how people spend their money on things they don't need, and don't know much about what they are getting, and buy it even without thinking ahead, you'd better go study rich folks. If I wasted money like that, I'd be dead.

—AFDC mother quoted in Newton (1977, p. 50)

This is the voice of an AFDC mother speaking to an economist who, after a year of being a participant-observer of poor people, concluded that poor people act rationally within their limited means (Newton, 1977). This chapter concerns issues related to money, and we conclude that poor consumers adapt to the financial realities with which they are faced. In this chapter, we discuss financial management by the poor and ways poor people obtain cash, pay bills, and carry out other financial transactions as alternatives to using banks. The chapter includes a description of money-saving techniques that are and are not used by poor consumers and concludes with a description of potential conflicts for marketers.

FINANCIAL MANAGEMENT BY POOR CONSUMERS

Financial management includes use of checking and savings accounts, automatic teller machines (ATMs), credit cards, loans, and other ways in

93

TABLE 6.1 Financial Management by Low-Income Households

Financial Vehicle	All Households	Household Income Less Than $20,000
Have checking account	82%	50%
Use ATM card	46	21
Use some credit card	77	44
Have had vehicle loan	59	27
Have had home equity loan	15	5

SOURCE: Metro Chicago Information Center (1994).

which people manage their money. Deregulation of financial services in the 1980s made banking more expensive or inconvenient for many poor people. For example, bank fees were raised; minimum balances were often required; and unprofitable branches, many of which were located in low-income neighborhoods, were closed ("They Will Gladly," 1992). There is also evidence that consolidation of banks through mergers has resulted in higher costs to the banking customer (Bradford & Cincotta, 1992).

The result of these changes is that 44% of those with annual incomes of less than $15,000 do not use banks (Belew, 1989), opposed to 19% of the general population. More than 80% of households without savings or checking accounts earned less than $20,000 (Joyal, 1992). Poor people offer various reasons for being "unbanked," ranging from insufficient funds to establish an account to insufficient financial management skills in managing a checkbook (Belew, 1989).

The Chicago area serves as an example of the lower use of mainstream financial management systems by poor people. Table 6.1 shows the percentage of people in the six-county Chicago area who use different financial services (Metro Chicago Information Center, 1994). It is clear that poor people in the Chicago area use mainstream financial services much less than more affluent people.

CREDIT UNIONS

An option for financial management by the poor is credit unions. Their advantage for low-income people is that they require only a low balance and offer "high-risk" loans. About 21% of low-income households use a credit union. Many low-income householders are simply not aware of credit unions as an alternative financial resource, however (Joyal, 1992).

CHECK-CASHING OUTLETS

The main financial management option open to poor people is the currency exchange, or check-cashing outlet. For a fee, these firms cash checks; issue money orders; sell postage stamps, food stamps, and lottery tickets; advance loans on income tax refunds; and perform electronic money transfers. Financial transactions are the core business of these firms.[1] The industry's 1990 fee income was $790 million ("They Will Gladly," 1992), and the number of check-cashing outlets grew from about 2,000 in 1987 to about 5,000 in 1993 (Hudson, 1993a). The fees are unregulated in 42 states (Hudson, 1993a) and vary widely; a check-cashing fee can be as high as 20% ("They Will Gladly," 1992).

On payday, you see long lines of the working poor waiting before the barred windows in currency exchanges. In the Chicago metropolitan area, only 8% of all people use currency exchanges to cash checks or pay bills, but 28% of people with an income of $20,000 or less do so (Metro Chicago Information Center, 1994). Currency exchanges are the main method of check cashing and bill payment for people who do not have checking accounts in the Chicago area (Metro Chicago Information Center, 1994). In Chicago, African Americans and Latinos are more likely to use currency exchanges and less likely to use banks than other consumers; 20% of Chicago residents use currency exchanges to pay their bills (Stangenes, 1993b). Despite higher costs compared to banks (Caskey, 1991a), check-cashing outlets offer advantages to poor consumers. They are conveniently located, have longer hours of business, are willing to assume risk, and offer multiple financial functions. Furthermore, because they are outside mainstream financial institutions, their transactions do not influence the credit ratings of their customers.

LOANS

Some financial firms specialize in loans to high-risk borrowers. A $50 billion market exists for "substandard" auto loans, and the higher rates of interest charged make this an attractive investment (Bary, 1994). In the South and Midwest, Mercury Finance Company specializes in loans to

people with low credit ratings. Such lenders carefully screen loan applicants to reduce their losses due to uncollectible loans (Stern, 1993) and
are increasingly using sophisticated and more accurate "risk-evaluation"
algorithms based on the extensive databases of financial transactions
currently available. This decreases the probability that a high-risk borrower will get a loan. Although this procedure should lower the cost to
low-income borrowers with good credit ratings, loan collectors are noto-
rious for their use of abusive and deceptive practices in attempting to
collect debts, despite limits set on their behavior by the Fair Debt
Collections Practice Act (see Higgins, 1993; Hill, 1994; Hudson, 1993b).

Another source of loans for people outside the mainstream financial system
is pawnshops. Pawnshops have several advantages: Clerks do not ask many
questions and do not ask for collateral other than the item being pawned,
and the transaction is quick. In 1988, pawnshops made about $1,723,000 in
loans, with an average loan of about $50 (Caskey, 1991b). Pawnshops in the
United States are almost all privately owned (unlike those in other nations,
which are run by charities) and are regulated by government. Regulation
covers aspects of the business such as filing police reports identifying the items
pawned and the individuals who pawned them, limitations on fees and
interest rates, and ownership of goods if a loan is defaulted on (Caskey,
1991b). A limitation to the use of pawnshops by low-income customers is
that they follow the same economic trends as do other financial institutions:
Credit is restricted in recessionary periods (Caskey, 1991b).

Pawnshops are more likely to be used by poor people. In order to examine
this hypothesis, we used the state as the unit of analysis and regressed the
percentage of people below the poverty level in 1992 (*Statistical Abstract of
the United States,* 1994) and the average disposable income in 1993 (*Statistical
Abstract of the United States,* 1994) against the estimated number of pawnshops in each state (Caskey, 1991b). We found that states with more
pawnshops have more people below the poverty level, as well as a lower level
of disposable income.[2] In an analysis of 28 states, Caskey (1991b) also found
that the number of pawnshops in a state was related to the proportion of the
population below the poverty level in the late 1980s.

OTHER FINANCIAL MANAGEMENT OPTIONS

An option for paying utility bills is through a bill collection system such
as Easy Pay or National Payments Network (NPN), both owned by

Western Union. They arrange to collect payments at neighborhood stores or convenience stores ("Customers Bank," 1991; "The Emerging Entrepreneur," 1990). The utility pays a fee for each utility payment, and the retailer is paid a transaction fee. All parties benefit: The retailer obtains customers who pay a bill at the retail store and may spend on other goods; customers pay bills conveniently and without a bank account; NPN or Easy Pay make a profit.

Another financial option is a prepaid card, such as the "secured" credit card, offered by firms such as Western Union. A secured credit card is like a debit card in that an amount equal to the credit line is deposited with the issuer. These cards, however, are expensive, with high annual fees and interest rates (Woolley, 1993b). Another type of prepaid card is a long-distance telephone card, which is issued in amounts ranging from $5 to $50 ("Western Union Offers," 1993).

ADDITIONAL COSTS

Poor consumers, without access to mainstream financial institutions or to electronic money transfers, also must bear the negative costs of a cash economy. One is the safety cost of carrying cash, which is particularly high in dangerous neighborhoods. Another cost of a cash economy is a lower inclination to keep records, which is likely to result in decreased control over financial resources. Furthermore, there is evidence that consumers categorize money from different sources in different ways (O'Curry, 1995). For example, consumers categorize cash as a more flexible medium of exchange than other forms of exchange such as credit cards or checks. Thus, people may easily divert cash designated for use in purchasing needed goods to other purposes (Kahneman & Tversky, 1979).

THE USE OF MONEY-SAVING TECHNIQUES BY LOW-INCOME HOUSEHOLDS

Low-income households use a number of techniques to save money. First, they tend to *spend on basic needs and fewer luxuries* and therefore purchase fewer products. For example, they scrimp on food and clothing, eat less than three meals a day, decide *which* child to buy clothing for, reduce resources for the home and auto, reduce use of services such as health and dental care, and cut back on entertainment and vacations. Second, they *change their shopping behaviors* by shopping at lower-cost outlets such as thrift shops and discount stores, doing more comparison shopping and bargain hunting, and emphasizing decision criteria such as durability and value. Third, they *change their financial management procedures*—that is, they may increase their use of credit, revise budgets and make special plans to pay bills, take out a second mortgage, sell items to keep other more desirable items, or use up savings (Caplovitz, 1981; Roberts, 1991; Wilhelm & Ridley, 1988).

These descriptions of money-saving tactics by poor consumers are supported by empirical evidence that less-affluent consumers are more price conscious. For example, Stephen Hoch's research on neighborhood differences in products purchased in a regional supermarket chain (Ryan, 1992) shows that blue-collar families in less-expensive houses are more concerned about discounts when they shop than are white-collar shoppers who live in neighborhoods with expensive homes. Furthermore, his research indicates that residents in areas with a low average level of education are likely to be more price sensitive in their supermarket shopping (Hoch, Kim, Montgomery, & Rossi, 1995).

COUPON USAGE

Coupons serve as another possible way to save money, but low-income households are less likely to use coupons (Bawa & Shoemaker, 1987; Blattberg & Neslin, 1990, p. 77; Levedahl, 1988). The 1991 Simmons Market Research Bureau, Inc. (1992) survey reports that households with annual incomes less than $10,000 are about 25% less likely to use coupons than the average household. Coupons offer value only to those who desire to buy the promoted brands, brands that are likely to be the category brand leaders and more expensive than store and generic brands. These brands may be attractive to income-constrained consumers because they are associated with quality. A person with little money could perceive name brands as offering the best value for their few dollars. This means that coupons for name brands should be seen as particularly attractive. Why, then, are they not likely to be used by poor consumers?

One possible reason for less coupon use by low-income households is that these consumers believe they can obtain both value and economy by buying store or generic brands of certain product categories. There are other possible reasons for low coupon use. For example, coupons are not as readily accessible to poor consumers. They are less likely to be received in the mail, and as less frequent readers of print media, poor consumers are less likely to encounter coupons in newspapers. It is also possible that low-income consumers are less-efficient coupon users in the sense that they are less able to locate, sort, organize, and cash in coupons (Levedahl, 1988).

Cultural differences also may play a role. Hispanics who identify with the Hispanic culture are reported to use coupons less frequently than Hispanics who identify with the mainstream U.S. culture (Exter, 1986). This is attributed to their brand loyalty (Schwartz, 1987) and to their belief that a coupon signals inability to pay, as the Spanish word *cupones* means both "coupons" and "food stamps" (LeRoux, 1987). They are also less exposed to coupons if they use Spanish media because many coupons are only printed in English ("Do Hispanic Shoppers," 1988; Donthu & Cherian, 1992). In fact, Hispanic households receive only 20 coupons compared to the 3,000 received by the average household annually (Fisher, 1990).

Thus, coupons, although a monetary inducement to purchase the popular brands favored by many consumers of all income levels, are not necessarily an accessible or a frugal option for saving money. In addition, with the current trend to decrease coupon face values, coupons may be even less attractive as a money-saving option.

GENERIC OR STORE-BRAND USAGE

Another way to save money is to use store or generic brands. Evidence from various sources indicates that poor consumers do not use generic or store brands more than do other consumers. There is a weak relationship between income level and use of generic supermarket products, according to a meta-analysis by Szymanski and Busch (1987), but generic products are bought by consumers of all income levels (Granzin, 1981). Some 1970s studies reported that low-income buyers preferred branded to private-label grocery items (e.g., Coe, 1971; French & Lynn, 1971; Murphy, 1978). The argument that private-label goods were new at the time and may have been unfamiliar to lower-income consumers is not true today, yet a 1984 study found that low-income consumers were still less likely to use generic products (McEnally & Hawes, 1984). In a simulated

TABLE 6.2 Usage of Generic and Store-Brand Products by Low-Income Households

Product	Percentage Use by All Households		Usage Index: Households With Less Than $10,000 Income	
	Generics	Store Brands	Generics	Store Brands
Paper towels	15.9%	13.1%	95	83
Aluminum foil	14.1	14.8	104	74
Paper napkins	14.8	12.4	82	55
Bleach	12.9	10.7	119	89
Plastic garbage bags	12.5	10.8	87	63
Sugar	12.4	13.2	118	73
Toilet paper	12.1	10.8	146	98
Dry pasta	9.3	10.2	78	93
Facial tissue	9.0	11.0	93	69
Canned vegetables	8.4	13.0	—	80
Canned fruit	7.7	10.8	—	68
Margarine	6.5	9.6	—	92
Frozen orange juice	6.2	11.1	—	62
Jams, jellies	6.2	8.5	—	90
Frozen vegetables	5.8	11.0	—	49
Cream cheese	4.8	8.0	—	47

SOURCE: Data from Simmons Market Research Bureau, Inc. (1992).

supermarket shopping study of African Americans, consumers did not increase their consumption of private-label and generic products even when prices of branded products were 40% higher (Whalen, 1981). Finally, the 1991 Simmons Market Research Bureau, Inc. (1992) survey indicates that low-income households are less likely than average to use generic or store brands (see Table 6.2). The exceptions are bleach, sugar, and toilet paper, which poor consumers are more likely to purchase in generic form than other households.

Generic products may not be used by poor consumers for several reasons. First, low-income consumers may be less aware of generic grocery products (Neidell, Boone, & Cagley, 1985). Second, until recently, generic grocery products were only labeled and had no identifying graphics or pictures. Low-income consumers are more likely to be functionally illiterate, and for those consumers who are functionally illiterate, generic products are indistinguishable from one another. Functional illiteracy is a problem of significance, affecting 16% of adult Whites, 44% of adult African Americans, and 56% of adult Hispanics (Whalen, 1983). Third, some generic products are of lower quality. Poor people who are conscious of the value purchased by their meager financial resources may be particularly aware of product performance differences and opt for branded products that are more effective. Fourth, low-income consumers may be loyal to well-known brands simply because they are familiar. Fifth, even low-cost generic products may be too expensive to use, for example, paper napkins. Or other products may be used as substitutes, such as paper towels for paper napkins or toilet tissue for facial tissue. Sixth, generic brands may not be available at the small grocery stores that are commonly located in poor neighborhoods. Seventh, nationally branded products may serve as a status symbol for consumers. In this case, only products that are less socially visible might be more likely to be purchased as generic brands.

Manufacturers of branded products do not seem to take appropriate marketing actions about the fact that poor consumers prefer branded products. The brand loyalty of poor consumers could be rewarded and encouraged by targeting poor consumers with coupons for these brands. If the product does indeed perform better than its competitors, this is to the advantage of both the manufacturer and the consumer.

AUTO MAINTENANCE

Another money-saving technique is performing your own car maintenance. Indeed, low-income households are more likely than more affluent households to fix their own cars: 26% of those with annual incomes less than $20,000 not only spend 6 hours or more a month working on their cars (Katcher, 1988) but also are more likely to patronize auto supply stores and other auto parts suppliers (Cavusgil, 1982). This is also due to the fact that they own older cars that need more maintenance.

SHOPPING AT LOW-PRICE OUTLETS

One might expect consumers from low-income households to make extensive use of stores that specialize in low-priced merchandise such as discount stores and warehouse stores. In fact, however, many of these stores are not used more by poor consumers.

In the recent past, discount stores *were* targeted at low-income consumers. For example, the typical 1980s Kmart customer used to be a blue-collar high school graduate with an income of $15,000 to $20,000 (Taub,

1983). Today, discount stores are promoted to and used by a broader range of income levels (Barnard, 1992; Dawson, Stern, & Gillpatrick, 1990; Gallagher, 1989). This is especially true during recessions and times of economic insecurity. Wal-Mart's success among some low-income consumers is partially due to their goals of satisfying customers with a level of service that reinforces the customer's self-respect. However, Wal-Mart's outlets are located outside urban areas, where they are less accessible to the most needy poor, who tend to be located in central cities.

Warehouse stores offer bulk merchandise at low prices and would seem to offer value to poor consumers. There are several barriers to their use by poor consumers. Poor households cannot afford to buy in bulk or stock up on sales items and often cannot store large amounts of product. There are also financial barriers. Warehouse stores often have membership fees that effectively exclude poor customers. In addition, some warehouse stores have the requirement, which poor people often cannot satisfy, of showing a driver's license and having a checking account ("Products No Longer," 1991; "The Wholesale Club Industry," 1988). Finally, these stores are often located near freeways and high-income areas (Gelbtuch, 1990), making them less accessible to inner-city low-income consumers.

Some stores are targeted to poor consumers who cannot afford the prices at discount stores like Wal-Mart or Kmart. These retail outlets specialize in offering low-priced irregular or closeout merchandise. Stores such as Bud's Warehouse Outlet, Dollar General, Family Dollar, Stuarts, and Kingsway are targeted to the downscale market (Dunn, 1986; Halverson, 1994; Stern, 1993). Dollar General, with 1,300 stores in the rural areas of 23 states, primarily sells irregular and closeout soft goods. These stores carry popular brand names, which appeal to low-income consumers just as they do to more affluent consumers. Bud's Warehouse Outlet is generally located in closed Wal-Mart stores. About 20% of its merchandise is surplus Wal-Mart merchandise, and the rest includes factory-refurbished goods returned because of defects and closeout merchandise (Halverson, 1994). Lerner's, a division of The Gap, has recently been renovated to appeal to low-income consumers (Bremner, 1990).

Although low-income households receive less advertising mail, at least one direct marketer, the Fingerhut catalog, targets lower-income households. It uses marketing approaches that are particularly attractive to consumers with limited resources, such as free gifts for customers who place large orders and installment plans for buying well-known brands, albeit at high interest rates (Schwabel, 1992).

Other sources of low-priced goods are merchandise outlets like Goodwill Industries or Salvation Army stores. The frequent patrons of these stores have lower incomes and shop there primarily for clothing and toys (Yavas & Riecken, 1981). One author has suggested that the quality of the goods available in these stores has diminished. This is because merchandise that used to be donated to social service organizations is often recycled to other middle-class consumers in garage sales (Gordon, 1985).

Another option is to participate in the informal economy, which involves bartering of services and goods, street vending, and flea markets. The primary appeal of flea markets, however, is not that they offer goods at low prices. Rather, they are frequented by consumers looking for entertainment—the excitement of barter, bargaining, and the chance of finding a treasure at a low price. There is also evidence that consumers of the informal economy tend to be more affluent, although the vendors may be less affluent (e.g., McCrohan, 1995; McCrohan & Smith, 1987; Razzouk & Gourley, 1982).

SUMMARY AND IMPLICATIONS

Poor consumers face barriers in managing their finances and must resort to special tactics to save money. On the other hand, marketers also face problems in their financial interactions with poor consumers.

Banks, like many other businesses in recent years, seek ways to run their business more efficiently and cost-effectively. As we have seen, one of the consequences of this legitimate business goal is the creation of barriers to poor consumers. From a marketer's point of view, there is an ethical conflict between running a profitable and efficient organization and the erection of barriers against the poorest portion of the population. Moreover, efficient operation does not require such barriers, and for this reason, government regulations require banking institutions to reinstitute poor consumers as customers, for example, through the Community Reinvestment Act.

Although financial transactions with the poor may carry higher risks, there are ways to reduce those risks. Efforts to educate low-income

consumers on financial management tactics have been somewhat successful in creating responsible use of, for example, credit cards (Bowers &
Crosby, 1980). Several banks have successfully offered limited checking
accounts in branches in low-income neighborhoods (Lunt, 1992). The
Union Bank in San Francisco has initiated its Cash & Save program with
services for low-income people, including check cashing and financial
service education (Major, 1994). Other options include on-line debit cards
for which the account is checked for funds at each transaction.

Alternative financial management organizations clearly provide a needed
service to poor consumers in today's society. There are just and unjust
alternatives to traditional banks. Just alternatives include bill collection
systems, credit unions, and prepaid secured credit cards. Unjust alternatives include those currency exchanges, pawnshops, and financial services
with excessive overcharge interest rates that use deceptive means to collect
loans (see Hudson, 1993b, for examples).

NOTES

1. Although some of these services are offered by, for example, a grocery store, the store
hopes to benefit from added sales of its core products (Caskey, 1991a).

2. Furthermore, as these two predictors independently contribute to the amount of
variability in the number of pawnshops in different states, people who are poor but above
the poverty level also appear to use pawnshops (R^2 adjusted = .19, $F(2,47)$ = 6.90, p = .002;
No. of pawnshops = 4.37 + .006 × poverty level − .00016 × disposable income level).

7

Promotion and Marketing Communications

> Every day, an unemployed single mother ritually views her regular
> daytime television "stories" and also sees many commercials. To her,
> this is as satisfying as visiting with good friends.

> A minister is arrested for tearing down billboard advertising for
> alcoholic beverages in Chicago's inner city.
>
> —Duff (1991)

Marketing communications are often the first and the most visible tools used by businesses to sell their goods. Yet, advertising by for-profit firms is sometimes considered unethical because it may make poor consumers desire material goods that are beyond their means (see, e.g., Pollay, 1986). In this chapter, we discuss several questions related to communication with poor consumers: How are poor consumers reached by marketing communications? Because they are avid television viewers, television receives special attention. What product categories advertising are targeted to poor consumers? How might marketing communications influence poor consumers? Are poor consumers at a disadvantage in interpreting marketing communications?

HOW ARE POOR CONSUMERS REACHED
BY MARKETING COMMUNICATIONS?

As a group, poor consumers are like other consumers in that they use all media that carry advertising—magazines, newspapers, radio, television, billboards, point-of-purchase displays, and telephone directory yellow pages. For example, low-income consumers report that they looked at about four magazines in the past 6 months, read two newspapers "yesterday," listen to about 3 hours of radio every day, and watch about 4 hours of television daily (Simmons Market Research Bureau, Inc., 1991). Compared to the average consumer, however, low-income consumers tend to watch more television and pay more attention to point-of-purchase advertising. At the same time, they read fewer magazines, newspapers, billboards, direct mail, and yellow pages. Figure 7.1 shows usage levels for marketing communication media by income (Simmons Market Research Bureau, Inc., 1991).

TELEVISION

Television is an important part of the lives of poor consumers. Compared to the rest of the public, more of them watch television, watch it for more hours, and value it more. People with low incomes are 30% more likely than average to watch television (Simmons Market Research Bureau, Inc., 1991). They are 21% more likely than average to be heavy television viewers (Simmons Market Research Bureau, Inc., 1991), watching a minimum of about 5 hours of television daily. Furthermore, a *TV Guide* survey indicates that 27% of people with an annual income of less than $20,000 think television is extremely important ("How Viewers Feel," 1993).

Not only do people with low incomes watch more television than people in the average household, but their viewing choices are different. The poor are particularly heavy viewers of daytime television, devoting a higher percentage of their viewing time to these programs compared to more affluent viewers (see Table 7.1). As only about one third of low-income households subscribe to cable TV (compared to more than half of all households), most of their TV viewing is of network and local free

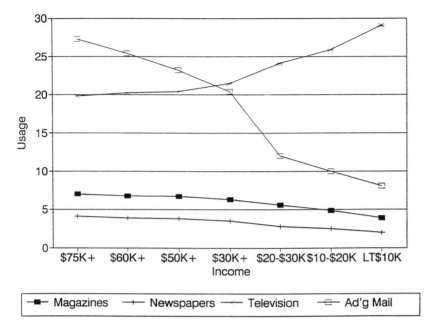

Figure 7.1. Media Usage by Income

SOURCE: Data from Simmons Market Research Bureau, Inc. (1991).
NOTE: Figures indicate average number of magazines read, average number of newspaper issues read yesterday, and average number of half hours viewed in 2 weeks of television.

television programming. Furthermore, adults from households with annual incomes under $10,000 are more likely than average to view "stories" such as situation comedies or soap operas. In contrast, affluent viewers with annual incomes of $40,000 or more are more likely to watch news and sports (Mediamark Research, Inc., 1993). Table 7.1 highlights differences in programs viewed by low and high income groups (Mediamark Research, Inc., 1993).

There are several possible reasons for the large role played by television in the lives of poor people. First, they have greater opportunity. More poor people are unemployed or retired and consequently spend more time at home where a television set is accessible. Second, they tend to have a lower level of education than the general population and are more likely to be

TABLE 7.1 Indexes of Viewing Specific Programs by High- and Low-Income
Viewers

	Income	
Program	Under $10,000	$40,000 or more
Daytime/Early evening		
Days of Our Lives, NBC	156	33
Guiding Light, CBS	149	29
Another World, NBC	144	22
One Life to Live, ABC	139	28
All My Children, ABC	123	45
The Young and the Restless, CBS	118	28
As the World Turns, CBS	116	24
Good Morning America, ABC	41	119
McNeil/Lehrer News Hour, PBS	54	153
Prime time		
Beverly Hills 90210, Fox	153	73
Herman's Head, Fox	147	93
Fresh Prince of Bel Air, NBC	136	64
Doogie Howser, M.D., ABC	134	99
Full House, ABC	134	72
Blossom, NBC	131	65
In Living Color, Fox	130	89
Wonder Years, ABC	130	103
Life Goes On, ABC	128	66
Married With Children, Fox	127	92
Dinosaurs, ABC	124	88
Step by Step, ABC	124	58
Quantum Leap, NBC	123	99
Seinfeld, NBC	121	128
This Old House, PBS	65	131
Cheers, NBC	105	123
Wings, NBC	111	122
Frugal Gourmet, PBS	68	115
Late night		
Comic Strip Live, Fox	137	90
Arsenio Hall, SYN	130	78
Tonight Show, NBC	88	133
News Nightline, ABC	81	132
Saturday Night Live, NBC	110	129
Program types		
Daytime dramas	135	33
Golf	51	195
Tennis	89	160
Football bowl games	102	155
Baseball specials	90	155
Football pro specials	94	150
Sports anthologies	86	130

SOURCE: Mediamark Research, Inc. (1993). Reprinted by permission.
NOTE: Includes programs viewed 15% more than average during 1992 by either of the two income groups.

functionally illiterate. Although functionally illiterate people have difficulty understanding written messages, they can readily take in messages from broadcast media such as radio or television. Third, television is one of the few recreational options that poor people can afford. Ownership of television sets and usage of television is virtually universal in this country.[1] Finally, television viewing is a safe form of entertainment in dangerous neighborhoods.

UNIQUE FEATURES OF TELEVISION ADVERTISING

Because low-income households are more likely to watch television, television advertising is expected to have a disproportionately large impact on them. Indeed, compared to more affluent people, those with incomes under $20,000 are more likely to believe that television advertising is authoritative (Russell & Lane, 1992). Low-income consumers consider broadcast media useful in helping them select products (Block, 1972), and some find it even more useful than print media (Schreiber & Boyd, 1980). An example of the impact of television advertising on consumer behavior is that poor consumers learned more about the link between consuming fiber from cereals and prevention of cancer after Kellogg introduced this linkage in an advertising campaign that included a lot of television advertising. After the start of this advertising campaign in 1984, the proportion of low-income adults who knew of this link increased more than fourfold and the proportion using fiber cereals increased threefold (Ippolito & Mathios, 1991).

To understand the effects of television advertising on poor consumers, we must consider how it differs from other forms of marketing communications. Because of its unique features, advertisers often use television advertising to accomplish different marketing communication goals than for other media. What are these unique features?

First, television advertising can effectively demonstrate a brand's use. In addition to "descriptive knowledge" about the advertised brand—what it is, how it looks, and who uses it—television advertising can provide "procedural knowledge" (Anderson, 1983; Stern, 1991) by dynamically demonstrating how the brand is used.

Second, in addition to providing verifiable information about brand attributes or benefits, television advertising is particularly well suited to communicating nonverifiable characteristics of a brand, such as the brand image or the image of the brand user. By use of symbolic techniques, including metaphor, allegory, and simile (Stern, 1988a, 1988b), television advertising can convey an image of the brand and allow the viewer to associate emotional responses to the brand. To understand television advertising, a viewer must know how to interpret these symbolic techniques.

Third, because television uses both visual and auditory channels and is a dynamic medium that changes over time, it offers the best media parallel to "real life." By sampling behavior in two sensory channels over time, the viewer can more easily interpret the meaning of the message. In contrast, print advertising, because it is solely visual and is capable of capturing only a moment in time, is not as rich in the information it can convey about time, location, and context. For this reason, the creative format of television advertising can be particularly persuasive.

In summary, the unique features of television make it particularly effective in allowing viewers to relate advertising and other messages to their own lives. Viewers learn how a product is functionally relevant to them and also how it can be socially and symbolically relevant to them.

There are two key implications of the uniqueness of television advertising for poor consumers: (a) Because television is such a large part of the lives of poor consumers, they are likely to be especially sophisticated about the techniques used to convey the functional, social, and symbolic messages in advertising; and (b) even when an advertising message is subtly presented, heavy television viewers, including poor consumers, are likely to be influenced by it because of the sheer number of times it is seen.

THE SPECIAL ROLE OF DRAMA ADVERTISING

Because it is a temporally dynamic medium, television advertising is well suited to telling a story, an event that unfolds over time. Stories are well-known to be effective persuasive techniques in many disciplines. For marketing communications, they are characterized as *drama advertising* (e.g., Deighton, Romer, & McQueen, 1989; Wells, 1989). Drama may be perceived as more "natural" because, as Deighton et al. (1989) noted, narrative is considered to be "logically prior to argument in human understanding" (p. 341).

Schank (1990) has proposed that

People think in terms of stories. They understand the world in terms of stories that they have already understood. New events or problems are understood by reference to old previously understood stories and explained to others by the use of stories. . . . Stories are very basic to the human thinking process. (p. 219)

"Understanding a story means being able to correlate the story we are hearing with one that we already know" (Schank, 1990, p. 21). Stories assume that the base for knowledge is common sense, derived from knowledge that one learns by experience by living in a culture (Lewis, 1987). Stories are based on "an unreflective, self-evidently 'true' set of beliefs" and are "what everyone knows" (Lewis, 1987, p. 292). In other words, you do not have to have a lot of schooling to have common sense. Because common sense, the basis for stories and other narrative discourse, is perceived as effortless, drama, too, may be perceived as easy to understand. It may be particularly easy to understand for people with less education, a common characteristic of poor people.

Drama advertising is an excellent creative approach for establishing brand and brand-user imagery and for describing how and in what situations a brand can be used. Low-income television viewers, who tend to watch stories in television programming rather than more informational programming, are likely to be able to easily interpret the communication techniques used in drama advertising.

There are several reasons that drama advertising can be particularly persuasive. First, a drama commercial, unlike a lecture commercial, requires the audience to draw its own conclusions. Drawing one's own conclusions results in more favorable beliefs about the advertised brand, more favorable brand attitudes, and a greater intent to purchase the advertised brand (Sawyer & Howard, 1991). One might expect that viewers who are more expert at interpreting drama advertising also may be more susceptible to its persuasive influences.

Second, drama advertising is more subtle in its brand message than is a nondramatic presentation of the message. This is because in drama advertising the message is inferred by the viewer from events in the plot and actions of the characters. In this creative approach, viewers are likely to use a "nonbrand" strategy to evaluate the commercial. When people use a nonbrand processing strategy for evaluating drama commercials, they do not evaluate the advertised brand directly although they may acquire information about it along with information about other aspects of the content of the commercial (Mitchell, 1983). The information they acquire may have an indirect effect on their evaluation of the brand because their attitude toward the *advertising* may influence their attitude about the *brand* (e.g., Lutz, Mackenzie, & Belch, 1983; Mitchell & Olson, 1981). Thus, another reason that drama advertising may be particularly effective is that viewers are less aware of its persuasive effects.

Third, drama advertising provides few cues to indicate to viewers that it is actually a marketing communication, compared to nondrama *lecture advertising,* which is directed at the audience like a speech. Whereas lecture commercials use cues such as voice-overs, talking heads, captions, and obvious brand presence, drama commercials may not be as easily categorized as commercial messages. As a result, viewers of drama commercials may be less likely or slower to use defensive consumer strategies (Friestad & Wright, 1994) to evaluate the messages.

Is drama advertising on television an inappropriate way to persuade a vulnerable population? We do not know enough to answer that question yet. Because drama advertising is more expensive, it is not used particularly frequently by advertisers. Also, it is often combined with the lecture format in a commercial. Furthermore, we do not know how well poor consumers use defensive strategies in viewing television advertising. As heavy television viewers, they are likely to be very familiar with persuasive television advertising techniques, and because they watch so much drama programming on television, they may be adept at interpreting television drama presentations. In addition, like the demographic age group called Generation X—people currently in their late teens and 20s who grew up watching a lot of television—they may be more cynical about television advertising than the general public (Howe & Strauss, 1992; Zinn, 1992). On the other hand, they may also be more susceptible to the persuasive influence of drama commercials, and a desire to obtain material goods may override their television advertising sophistication.

MAGAZINES AND NEWSPAPERS

Although magazines and newspapers are less likely to be read in low-income than other households, they are not completely absent. Only 9% of adults from low-income households (below $20,000 a year) are among the heaviest 20% of newspaper readers. Similarly, only 14% of these low-income household members are among the heaviest 20% of magazine readers (Simmons Market Research Bureau, Inc., 1991).

One reason that poor consumers are less likely to use magazines and newspapers is that more of them are functionally illiterate. Functional

TABLE 7.2 Likelihood That Low-Income Consumers Will Always Refer to Point-of-Purchase Communications

Communication	Percentage of All Consumers Who Always Refer	Index: Households With Less Than $10,000 Annual Income
Food stores		
Overhead aisle marker	19.2	108
Shelf messages	8.5	125
Shopping cart ads	3.9	163
Store flyers	20.0	108
Coupon centers	4.5	136
Public announcements	4.2	126
Demonstrations	5.7	120
Samples	8.1	123
Nonfood stores		
Aisle markers	19.9	99
Shelf/rack signs	16.6	110
Shopping cart ads	3.5	158
Store flyers	17.6	93
Public announcements	5.6	141
Video monitor displays	2.6	127
Lighted merchandise graphics	3.5	108

SOURCE: Data from Simmons Market Research Bureau, Inc. (1991).

illiteracy in this country is estimated to be as high as 28%. As Whalen (1983) pointed out, a functionally illiterate consumer can understand only the pictorial part of print advertising and is less able to use coupons. With the increase in growth of ethnic populations in the United States with a language other than English, functional illiteracy in English has become a problem of some concern to marketers.

POINT-OF-PURCHASE ADVERTISING

Poor consumers are more likely to use point-of-purchase marketing communications than are more affluent consumers. Point-of-purchase communications include messages or offers at the shelf; on the shopping cart; and in in-store public announcements, demonstrations and samples, coupon centers, and computerized information, as well as through a highly visible store location (Simmons Market Research Bureau, Inc., 1991). Table 7.2 indicates the use of various point-of-purchase communications by poor consumers relative to the average consumer.

Why is point-of-purchase marketing communication such a strong influence on poor consumers? One possible reason is that it is one of the main opportunities for poor consumers to gather information. Because they are less likely to get information about product and brand prices from newspapers, poor consumers may use point-of-purchase information to compare brands, prices, and values. A second possible reason is that poor consumers may not plan their purchases ahead of time. However, Zeithaml (1985) reports that low-income consumers actually plan more than the average consumer and are more likely to use shopping lists. Even point-of-purchase communications can be a problem for functionally illiterate people, however. They find it difficult to use generic products that lack pictures and are handicapped in using guides to distribution locations such as nonpictorial store signage (Whalen, 1983).

DIRECT MAIL

In 1991, the advertising mail received by the average household was more than half of all of the mail delivered (U.S. Department of Labor, Survey of Labor Statistics, 1992). But poor households get only about one quarter of the advertising mail received by the most affluent households. Table 7.3 shows the number of pieces of first- and third-class advertising mail received per week by income (U.S. Department of Labor, Survey of Labor Statistics, 1992). Perhaps because they receive less mail, poor consumers are more likely to read it. About one quarter of people with annual incomes under $10,000 reported in 1991 that they usually read advertising mail, compared to an average of 15% for all households (U.S. Department of Labor, Survey of Labor Statistics, 1992). This mail is welcomed by poor consumers; it is the more affluent consumers who prefer to get less advertising mail (U.S. Department of Labor, Survey of Labor Statistics, 1992).

Although direct mail is used for marketing communications by some stores that target low-income consumers (Dunn, 1986), low-income consumers are not typical targets for direct marketing. This medium would seem to have potential not only for marketers of for-profit goods but also for social services.

OUTDOOR ADVERTISING

Outdoor advertising is generally used by advertisers to remind consumers of their brands. By its nature, it is not appropriate for intensive

TABLE 7.3 Pieces of First- and Third-Class Advertising Mail Received per Week by Income, 1991

Income	Total Pieces of Advertising Mail
Under $7000	7.0
$7,000-$9,999	9.2
$10,000-$14,999	9.5
$15,000-$19,999	10.5
$20,000-$24,999	11.8
$25,000-$29,999	12.2
$30,000-$34,999	14.1
$35,000-$49,999	15.2
$50,000-$64,999	16.7
$65,000-$79,999	21.4
$80,000-$99,999	27.2
$100,000 or more	27.5

SOURCE: U.S. Department of Labor, Survey of Labor Statistics (1992).

informational messages and often contains only one or two informational cues, such as availability or attributes (Taylor & Taylor, 1994). Tobacco products account for the most spending on outdoor advertising, with retail stores and alcohol products second and third (Leading National Advertisers, Inc., 1991). People with low incomes are as likely to see billboards as the average consumer (Simmons Market Research Bureau, Inc., 1991), but because they use public transportation more than more affluent people, they are more likely to be exposed to transit advertising. Transit advertising in buses and subways often is used to reach low-income consumers in urban areas by public service providers but is less used by businesses.

OTHER WAYS OF COMMUNICATING WITH POOR CONSUMERS

In addition to television and point-of-purchase communications, more informal communication channels may be used by poor consumers. Word-of-mouth information gathered informally from other people may be a particularly trustworthy channel of communication for people who are outside of or have learned to distrust the mainstream of society. Word of mouth may include communications with individuals as well as with organizations. Word-of-mouth communications influence stores visited, products purchased (Dunn, 1986), and social service programs used (Hirst & Talwar, 1981).

Some businesses are aware of word of mouth as a marketing communication channel. For example, Union Bank of San Francisco does "grassroots marketing" of its check-cashing service by working with Hispanic organizations and participating in local events (Major, 1994). Similarly, Coors beer, by contributing to Hispanic community organizations (Maxwell & Jacobson, 1989), hopes to develop a more positive image in the community on the basis of word-of-mouth communication.

What of marketing communication media on the horizon? Marketers are starting to use electronic marketing to make consumers aware of their products as well as to distribute products. The use of graphics on the World Wide Web on Internet is increasingly attracting national as well as smaller firms. Currently, the people with the equipment and interest to use this form of electronic marketing are primarily affluent, young, male, and technically inclined. As access to the electronic market becomes easier, however, the audience will become more diverse. Unfortunately, poor people are unlikely to be part of this audience. They will not have the hardware or the expertise to gain access to the electronic marketplace, even when it becomes a marketplace for products they can use. They cannot afford the computers, the modems, or the phone lines. Their older neighborhoods are not likely to be provided with the infrastructure required to support the electronic market. Their schools do not have the hardware, software, or personnel to teach poor children how to use computers, let alone computer communications.

SUMMARY OF HOW POOR CONSUMERS ARE REACHED BY MARKETERS

In summary, the poor are more likely to learn about goods from television advertising; point-of-purchase communications; and possibly word of mouth from friends, relatives, and neighbors. Characteristics common to these three means of communicating are the following:

- They are *fleeting* (television and conversation are dynamically temporal media; signage or product location in stores is noted in passing).
- They often *rely less on written language* than other communication formats.
- They are *perceived as "free"* (television because the cost of the set and power to run it are not thought of as part of the cost of viewing; point-of-purchase communications because their cost is hidden in the cost of products)

compared to newspapers and magazines for which consumers pay by the issue.

The most effective television messages may be couched as drama advertising, a format familiar to and likely to be easily understood by poor consumers. Although poor consumers may be particularly susceptible to drama television advertising, they may well have developed effective ways of coping with this persuasive technique. An approach to thinking about this issue is discussed later in this chapter.

Direct mail, if it can be ensured of delivery in low-cost multidwelling housing, may be an effective communication medium because it is underused for this population.

WHO ADVERTISES
TO LOW-INCOME CONSUMERS?

The amount a firm spends on advertising a brand depends on influences such as its marketing and marketing communication goals, the stage in the brand's life cycle, the budget, and the product category. Marketers may choose to direct marketing messages about a product, such as home permanents or cigarettes, to low-income consumers, but not all marketing communications directed at low-income consumers are intended for them. In an effort to save money, some marketers advertise their brands on daytime television and *inadvertently* direct that advertising to low-income consumers (Fulgoni, 1988).

To determine the product categories likely to be advertised on television to low-income viewers, we examined a sample of commercials aired during seven television programs viewed by many poor consumers (see Table 7.4). Television advertising aired during the seven daytime drama programs is likely to be watched by a high proportion of low-income viewers. Three hundred thirty-seven commercials were aired during these programs on one day in December 1994. This sample of commercials is obviously biased by the seasonal influences of cold weather and the holiday season, with more commercials for cold remedies and gifts, but it also includes commercials for products that are less seasonally influenced.

The sample of commercials is notable for what is missing as much as for what is present. Soap operas are named for the cleaning products that

TABLE 7.4 Television Advertising During Seven Daytime Programs Heavily Viewed by Low-Income People

Product Category	Number of Commercials	Percentage of Total
Total	337	100%
Food and drink	67	20
Personal care	40	12
Medication and vitamins	31	9
Household cleaners and detergents	25	7
Durable products	21	6
Retail outlets	20	6
Fragrances	18	5
Toys—child and adult	16	5
Baby products	12	4
Clothing	10	3
Television programs	42	12
Other	30	9

used to be their dominant sponsors, but cleaning products are no longer the most heavily advertised product category during these daytime television programs (see Table 7.4). Rather, food products such as cookie dough, cereal, and snacks like chips and popcorn account for 20% of the commercials. Personal care products such as facial lotion, feminine hygiene products, cosmetics, hair care products, and bath soaps account for 12%. Medications such as cough medicine, lip balms, pain relievers, and vitamins account for 9% of the commercials, and household or laundry cleaning products account for 7% of the commercials. In comparison, advertising during prime time included commercials for beer, vehicles, and financial products as well as for some of the same products advertised during daytime programming.

What about advertising in other media? Advocates for the poor contend that sin products such as liquor and cigarettes are particularly targeted to low-income consumers. For example, rap musicians have been used to market malt liquor to inner-city African Americans and Hispanics ("Malt Liquors," 1992).

There is evidence of a disproportionately high number of billboards for alcohol and tobacco products in poor neighborhoods in several locations: A Chicago Lung Association study found three times as many tobacco billboards and five times as many alcohol billboards in poorer and predominately minority city wards than in predominately White city wards (Duff, 1991).

A systematic content analysis of billboards in 20 zip code areas in each of two cities, Detroit and San Antonio, reported a higher proportion of alcohol and tobacco billboard advertising in low- and middle-income than in high-income zip code areas (Lee & Callcott, 1994). As a proportion of all billboard advertising in Detroit and San Antonio, alcoholic beverages accounted for 8.9% and tobacco for 23.1%. In Detroit, alcohol billboards accounted for 13.7% and tobacco for 26.3% of billboards.

In comparison, although the methodology is somewhat different, a study of billboards on federally funded highways throughout Michigan found that 3.3% were for alcoholic beverages and 4.5% were for tobacco products (Taylor & Taylor, 1994).

As reported in Chapter 5, in 1989, 70% of more than 2,000 billboards in the city of Baltimore advertised alcohol or tobacco products, and three fourths of them were in poor neighborhoods ("Distilling the Truth," 1992). Thus, there is evidence that alcohol and tobacco tend to be advertised on billboards more heavily in low-income areas.

Targeting poor consumers for these products has not gone unnoticed. When a brand of cigarettes was targeted at low-income women, public outcry caused them to be withdrawn from the market. Some municipal and state governments have legislated against advertising of certain sin products. Several cities and states (Maryland and Utah) do not allow tobacco ads in public transportation, and Baltimore restricts tobacco and alcohol advertising in outdoor locations (Bird, 1994).

In summary, although billboards are inappropriately used to advertise sin products, television commercials are used for products that are not unreasonable to advertise to low-income consumers. Marketers who use television to target low-income consumers during the programs they are likely to watch are effectively using accepted marketing tools of segmentation and targeting.

ARE THE POOR AT A DISADVANTAGE
IN INTERPRETING MARKETING COMMUNICATIONS?

It has been argued that advertising in mass media unduly raises the aspirations of poor consumers for material goods (Pollay, 1986)—that is, by supporting materialism as a key cultural value, advertising can frustrate people who have few financial resources. Are poor consumers particularly vulnerable to marketing communications?

In the past, the behavior of low-income consumers has been described as "more receptive to advertising that depicts activity . . . and solutions to practical problems in daily life and social relationships" (Berkman & Gilson, 1976, p. 652). Also, poor people purportedly get information best through visual sources. Finally, lower-class consumers were characterized as impulsive and poorly organized shoppers.

Evidence presented in this chapter could be interpreted to support those early descriptions and to suggest that poor consumers are more vulnerable to persuasion by marketing communications. Because poor consumers watch a lot of television, they might be characterized as more "visual," and because they rely a lot on point-of-purchase information, they might be characterized as more impulsive shoppers. But it is important to recognize that poor people use more television and point-of-purchase information not only because of personal reasons but also because of their circumstances.

One circumstance that influences the action of poor consumers is that they view more television because they have a greater opportunity. Another is that poor people may be particularly susceptible to in-store marketing communications because they lack experience with a variety of distribution outlets. Poor consumers tend to shop in their neighborhoods. Their lack of experience with a variety of stores and salespeople limits their effectiveness in comparing and evaluating sales tactics.

The idea that poor people have certain cognitive or personality traits that influence their consumer skills is discussed in Chapter 4. These traits include a tendency to believe they have little control over their own fate. If you believe you have little control over your own fate, you may be less critical and less well defended against marketing communications. Thus, poor consumers may be less likely to use effective tactics for coping with persuasion because they do not believe they have sufficient control over their fate to do so. In addition, poor people tend to use a cognitive style that is less effective for coping with persuasive communications—they tend to be "simplifiers," rejecting incongruous information rather than seeking information to clarify what they know (Schaninger & Sciglimpaglia, 1981).

There are also reasons to believe that poor consumers are quite capable of resisting persuasive marketing communications. As mentioned earlier, because they view a lot of television advertising, they should be familiar with and sophisticated about coping with television's persuasive tactics.

Also, to survive, they know they must stretch every dollar, so they should be primed to resist persuasive marketing communication tactics. They should be especially sensitive to communications about value and price.

A THEORETICAL FRAMEWORK

Although we can speculate about the ability of poor consumers to cope with marketing communications, we do not have empirical evidence about how well poor consumers cope with the persuasiveness of marketers. We can describe what coping tactics might be like. Friestad and Wright (1994) offer a theoretical model for describing the critical components of people's tactics for coping with persuasive communications.

If poor consumers are able to effectively cope with persuasive communications, this model suggests that they should use several tactics. Those tactics include the following:

- Less cognitive effort in processing the persuasive messages
- Better ability to recognize persuasive aspects of marketing communications
- Better ability to make inferences about the marketer's motivations
- Better ability to remember how they have coped with persuasive situations in the past

In addition, people who are effective in coping with persuasive tactics must be aware of the nonverbal as well as the verbal cues used by advertisers to create impressions. For example, how much are poor consumers aware that nonverbal cues such as attractiveness, fashionable clothing, and clothing appropriate to the role played by the model are used to invoke trust in a spokesperson?

People who are effective in coping with persuasive tactics also should know that simply being familiar with a spokesperson, a commercial, or an advertising campaign may lead to liking the brand (Bornstein, 1989; Zajonc, 1968). The persuasive message may be not understood or may even be ignored, but its mere exposure can lead to a favorable attitude to the advertised brand.

If poor consumers are less effective at coping with persuasive marketing communications, Friestad and Wright's (1994) model suggests that as "novice consumers," they would have other reactions to marketing communications:

- They would be more likely to agree with rigid classifications such as, "All TV ads are misleading."
- They would be more likely to deny that persuasion is taking place if it is presented by someone they do not think of in that role (e.g., Michael Jordan).
- They would have an intense positive (or negative) reaction to all ads with a particular persuasion tactic.
- They would depend more on other people's reactions to a marketing message and be more likely to display public emotional reactions during persuasion situations.

SUMMARY AND IMPLICATIONS

Much business promotion is communicated through mass media such as television, radio, print, and outdoor advertising. By definition, mass media do not address a closely selected audience. It can only be roughly tuned to reach the people who are most likely to purchase the advertised brand. It would seem to be unreasonable to suggest that the exposure of advertising via mass media to *unintended* audiences, which might include poor consumers, should or can be the sole responsibility of marketers.

Aside from the billboard advertising of tobacco and alcohol products, marketers appear to follow accepted marketing practices in their communications with consumers. They strive to expose their messages to the audiences most likely to purchase their brands. This means, for example, advertising "care" products such as baby products and medications on daytime television when caretakers are likely to be reached. This also means advertising motor vehicle, financial, and computer and telecommunication products during prime-time television or in other media likely to reach more affluent people.

Marketers use a variety of techniques to present their brands in the most favorable light, to communicate information and image about their brands, and to persuade consumers to purchase a promoted brand. They vary these techniques depending on characteristics of the audience, such as educational level. They also vary the content of their communications depending on characteristics of the target audience. In general, national advertisers do not appear to go out of their way to be deceptive in their marketing communications.

At the same time, poor consumers may cope quite well with marketing communications. Until clear evidence is presented that poor people are especially vulnerable to persuasive marketing communications, neither marketers nor regulators have a need or an incentive to paternalistically protect them.

NOTE

1. More than 96% of households with incomes under $10,000 own a TV set (Simmons Market Research Bureau, Inc., 1991, p. 376).

8

Price Discrimination and Retail Markets

The Lake Worth grandmother left . . . work . . . to catch the bus to the Publix [supermarket]. "It's exhausting, it's definitely inconvenient," Marshall said. "But I have to do what I have to do." . . . Since January when the Winn-Dixie near her home closed, Marshall has had no supermarket within walking distance of her home. . . . If she runs short of food during the week, she has to buy from neighborhood convenience stores. "I buy milk and cereal sometimes but no real groceries because you really can't afford that," she said. After checking out at Publix, Marshall had a clerk call her a cab. The 3.2-mile ride to her house . . . cost $5.75.

—Fields (1995)[1]

In the past four chapters, we focused on problems of poor consumers; the products they purchase; their sources of and access to financial resources, financial management techniques, and money-saving opportunities; and their communications with marketers. In this chapter, we examine the characteristics of the marketplace that serves disadvantaged consumers.

Research on this topic in the 1960s and 1970s focused on price differentials between poor consumers and the rest of the population (see Andreasen, 1978, for a review). We begin this chapter with a discussion of the sources of differences in prices for poor and nonpoor consumers. These differences take both pecuniary and nonpecuniary forms; that is, they are both direct prices charged to a customer and indirect nonmonetary costs to the customer. In many instances, differences are due to characteristics of poor consumers themselves as well as the organization of retail markets in predominantly poor areas.

Much of this chapter is relevant to poor consumers who live in predominantly poor areas. The reason for this limitation is that the opportunity for a business to discriminate in pricing is partially a function of the structure of the marketplace. For this reason, we focus on the differences in retail establishments in poor and nonpoor areas. Although not all poor consumers are subject to the same market forces, a substantial portion are segregated geographically.

Not all poor consumers live in predominantly low-income areas. As documented in Chapter 4, families living outside of metropolitan areas face a higher probability of living in poverty than do their urban cousins. Fully 75% of the poor in the United States live in metropolitan areas, however, and 42.4% live in the central cities.

The percentage of the poor that live in inner-city poverty areas is a minority of the poverty population, but there is evidence that this group is increasing in size. Danziger and Gottschalk (1987) noted a substantial increase in the concentration of poverty in very poor areas between 1969 and 1979 for both Blacks and non-Blacks. At a more aggregate level, the central city, Blank (1993) reports that the percentage of the poor living in central cities increased slightly between 1964 and 1990, from 32.8% to 35.2%.

PRICE DIFFERENTIALS

Prices paid by poor consumers may differ from those paid by other consumers for a number of reasons. Poor consumers may face higher prices at the retail outlet due to their household characteristics (e.g., household size or composition). For example, poor households may be unable to take advantage of quantity discounts because of their low income, and their market basket of goods and services may be more expensive due to the mix of commodities. The characteristics of the marketers serving the poor community (e.g., store size and operating costs) also may cause the poor to face higher prices. Furthermore, for goods of the same retail price, the poor may be offered lower-quality merchandise and different credit arrangements, leading to higher effective prices for them. Lastly, the poor also may bear higher nonmonetary costs for purchasing items than nonpoor consumers. For example, it may take longer to travel to a retail outlet.

In 1975, Andreasen (1975) carefully examined direct monetary price differences between neighborhoods in the inner city, whether prices in poorer neighborhoods are generally higher; whether they are higher only for certain products; whether they are higher in independent, nonchain stores; and whether they are higher on the day welfare checks arrive. He found that poor consumers pay higher prices for both durable and nondurable goods.

Several recent studies suggest that Andreasen's findings are still valid in today's marketplace. For example, a comparison of poor- and middle-class neighborhoods in two California cities in 1992 found that food costs in a poor Los Angeles community were 15% to 28% higher than in a middle-class Los Angeles community (Consumers Union, 1993, p. 43). A 1991 study of New York City neighborhood food shopping found that the poor faced food costs almost 9% higher than those borne by middle-income shoppers (New York City Department of Consumer Affairs, 1991). Supermarket chains sometimes segment their stores by price zones with different prices. In one study of a large supermarket chain in the Chicago area, it was found that the price zones were assigned on the basis of the level of local competition (Hoch et al., 1995). For poor neighborhoods, which have little competition from other supermarkets or from warehouse stores, this leads to higher prices.

Just as in the 1970s, groceries are not the only products for which the poor face higher prices. There are price differentials in banking, insurance, and durable goods as well. The California comparison of low- and middle-income consumers found that low-income consumers tend to pay higher bank fees than do middle-income consumers (Consumers Union, 1993). In particular, bank fees are structured to encourage large account balances. Poor consumers often cannot maintain the required minimum average balances and therefore pay higher fees, such as charges for each check written. In addition, because few bank branches are located in poor neighborhoods, many low-income bank customers must face higher transaction costs in travel costs to and from their bank.

Poor consumers often pay more for durable goods as well. Because poor consumers often do not have the cash to pay for durables outright and find it difficult to obtain installment credit, they do business with retail outlets that lease durable goods such as television sets, washing machines, and furniture. These firms are convenient, offer friendly service, allow a customer to avoid legal contracts, and allow immediate use of a product without a layaway plan (Hudson, 1993b). In the words of one customer, "The prices could be cheaper but they treat me like I'm a somebody" (Freedman, 1993, p. A1).[2] Because formal credit is frequently unavailable to poor consumers, leasing is often the only alternative.

Yet in the long run, leasing goods carries high penalties. Firms charge high leasing rates; markups equivalent to annual interest rates of 231% have been reported (Freedman, 1993), and products can be repossessed if a payment is missed (Woolley, 1993a). Because three quarters of customers miss payments, repossession must make a substantial contribution to the profitability of this business and represents a substantial loss to poor consumers. The business of leasing durable goods is not regulated at the federal level, and it is covered by only limited regulation at the state level (Woolley, 1993a).

Even when poor consumers are able to obtain credit, they often are required to purchase credit insurance. This "insurance" guarantees the lender payment if the purchaser is unable to meet payments. Some lenders have purportedly forced borrowers to take out this insurance, although this requirement is illegal; others overcharge for the insurance (Hudson, 1993a). This type of insurance is expensive to the consumer: "While other types of insurance typically pay 70 cents in claims for every dollar collected in premiums, credit insurers pay an average of only 42 cents" (Hudson, 1993a, p. 25). Insurers also have been accused of practicing redlining in refusing to offer insurance coverage or offering limited coverage in low-income (and often high-crime) neighborhoods (Brostoff, 1993; Woolley, 1993a).

PRICE DISCRIMINATION
VERSUS PRICE DIFFERENTIALS

In sum, poor consumers still pay more for groceries, face unfavorable banking fees, and often pay more for durable goods. The higher prices paid by poor consumers are not necessarily evidence of price discrimination, however. Price discrimination occurs when the same product is sold at more than one price or, more accurately, when a product of identical production, marketing, and distribution costs is sold at different prices. To the extent that firms serving poor communities face higher costs of business and pass these costs on to consumers, the poor face higher prices but not price discrimination.

The term *price discrimination* is frequently taken to be synonymous with *price differential* in studies examining prices in poor versus nonpoor communities. As the preceding definition makes clear, the two are not necessarily the same, although the ability of a marketer to discriminate in pricing depends on the same factors as the ability to charge different prices and has the same effect on the consumer. The distinction between discrimination and differential is important as a basis for evaluating whether the higher prices charged to poor consumers are based on real market costs.

Price discrimination is generally considered legal in the United States except to the extent that it lessens competition.[3] Not only is it legal to charge different prices for otherwise similar goods that have different costs of production, marketing, and distribution, it is also legal to do so for goods that have identical total costs as long as it does not lessen competition in the marketplace. Economic theory predicts that firms will discriminate in pricing, when possible, to maximize profits.[4]

From a businessperson's perspective, many forms of price discrimination are both legal and viewed as positive ways to increase the profitability of the firm. For example, firms often send coupons of different face value to customers of different desirability to them. Higher face values are sent to customers the firm wants to win over because they are not consistent users or loyal to that firm's brand.

CONDITIONS CONDUCIVE TO PRICE DISCRIMINATION/DIFFERENTIATION

The question is, then, what marketplace characteristics allow for price discrimination or differentiation? The ability of a firm to discriminate in pricing is determined by two factors, both of which are necessary but neither of which is alone sufficient. The ability of a firm to charge different prices for similar goods requires (a) identifiable differences in consumers' price sensitivity and (b) the ability to isolate markets. If marketers can

isolate individuals less sensitive to changes in price for a good or service
from the rest of the marketplace (for whatever reason), they will be able
to charge higher prices to these consumers. The following discussion
examines these two requirements.

PRICE SENSITIVITY AND PRICE ELASTICITY OF DEMAND

Consumers' responsiveness to price is measured by what economists
term their *price elasticity of demand*. This measure quantifies the percentage
change in the quantity demanded of a good for a percentage change in a
good's price. The notion of price elasticity of demand recognizes that price
increases reduce the quantity demanded of a product, all else being equal.
Price elasticity refers to the level of the response to a change in price. The
more price elastic the demand for a good, the greater the response in the
quantity demanded for a given change in price. When consumers are very
sensitive to a good's price, the price cannot include a high markup.[5]
Therefore, a necessary, but not sufficient, condition for marketers to
discriminate in pricing against poor consumers for particular commodities
requires that poor consumers be less sensitive to price changes for the
goods (i.e., have lower price elasticities of demand).

Several factors influence the price elasticity of demand for a particular
commodity, including consumer income, the proportion of total income
spent on a given good, the availability of substitute goods, and whether
consumers are slow to change their buying habits. In theory, for goods for
which demand increases with an increase in income, such as automobiles and
ice cream, consumers with higher incomes are expected to have higher price
elasticities. The reason for this seemingly counterintuitive relationship is that
people with higher incomes have greater options and are more able to
substitute alternative goods or to travel to make price comparisons. Conversely, people with lower incomes should be less price sensitive to the extent
that they find it difficult to substitute alternative goods or they cannot travel
to a vendor with lower prices. As the percentage of total income spent on a
particular good increases, price elasticity of demand increases. This reflects
the greater importance of the item in the consumer's decisions. For example,
consumers do more price comparing for housing than for a bar of soap.

How price sensitive are poor consumers compared to the balance of
the population? Factors that would make them less price sensitive include
decreased access to alternative retail outlets, a tendency not to substitute

for more expensive goods, and slowness to change their buying habits. All of these factors would also increase poor consumers' susceptibility to price discrimination. A factor that would make them more price sensitive is spending a high proportion of their financial resources on necessities such as food and housing. Price sensitivity of poor consumers is likely to vary by product or service category. It would be expected that the net effect of these factors on price discrimination for basic foodstuffs and housing is influenced by the large percentage of total expenditures that the poor allocate to these items. For items like clothing, however, the predicted effects suggest that due to lower incomes and the fewer available substitutes, the poor should have lower price elasticities of demand and therefore may be subject to price discrimination.

MARKET ISOLATION

The second requirement for price discrimination is market isolation. If the poor are able to shop at the same outlets as the nonpoor, marketers will be unable to identify and isolate them for price discrimination; to the extent that poor consumers are restricted geographically in their choice of merchants, they may be effectively isolated.

An alternative for low-income consumers is to shop outside the local neighborhood—"outshopping." Most studies find that outshoppers tend to be more affluent consumers (Haws & Lumpkin, 1984), probably because low-income shoppers face transportation problems in getting out of their local community. Poor consumers also may face language and social barriers when they venture out of their local communities.

Nonetheless, the Consumers Union (1993) study of several California communities found that poor families are more likely to seek basic goods and services outside their neighborhoods, quite possibly due to the higher prices charged locally, the lower-quality goods, or the lack of providers in their neighborhoods. In the California study, only one third of money used for food shopping was spent by low-income families in their own neighborhoods, compared to 83% by middle-class families (Consumers Union, 1993, p. 28). This outcome is consistent with the previous argument due to the higher percentage of total expenditures accounted for by food expenditures.

Affluent consumers simply assume they will be able to obtain goods and services for their everyday needs near where they live because this is an accepted norm in our society. For example, the study of California neighborhoods pointed out that most of the money spent for food shopping by middle-class households was spent in their own neighborhoods. Also satisfied were their needs for services such as banking, laundromats, dry cleaning, and general shopping (Consumers Union, 1993). Not only are more affluent people more likely to shop in their own neighborhoods, but because they usually have cars, they also have easier access to retail outlets outside their neighborhoods.

Poor people do not enjoy such convenient access to the products they need. For virtually every one of their daily needs, poor consumers must either shop at stores in inconvenient locations or obtain goods at higher prices in local stores. For example, Michael Porter (1995) reports that in Los Angeles, "Retail penetration per resident in the inner city is 35% of the rest of the city in supermarkets, 40% in department stores, and 51% in hobby, toy and game stores" (p. 58).

When there are no or few conveniently located outlets for consumers to shop at or obtain services, they have two alternatives. Either they obtain their needs at less-convenient locations, generally outside their neighborhoods, or they patronize the few local outlets. Commonly, it has been found that prices tend to be higher when there are a limited number of outlets in a neighborhood (e.g., Andreasen, 1975; Bell & Burlin, 1993).

Nonmonetary Costs

When poor consumers must fulfill basic needs outside the immediate locale, travel costs and travel time must be added to the costs of goods and services. As described in Chapter 5, people from low-income households are heavy users of public transportation, spending half again as much as the average household on public transportation (Ambry, 1993). Yet, the poor are not always well served by public transportation, and when public transportation is eliminated, the poorest residents are the ones most often affected. As alternatives to public transportation, the poor use taxicabs or car pools for which the driver charges a fee. Other nonpecuniary costs that may be borne by poor consumers are costs for translators when non-English speakers need to carry out transactions with institutions such as banks. There can also be psychological costs. In addition, users of food stamps often suffer the disdain of cashiers and other customers (Polakow, 1993; Rank, 1994). When a food stamp user noted that supermarket cashiers always seem to replenish the supply of change when they discover he is using food stamps, another customer responded that this was how they were making him pay his way (Rank, 1994).

THE STORES THAT SERVE POOR NEIGHBORHOODS

With fewer large retail outlets, consumers are often limited to shopping at local small grocery, or mom-and-pop, stores. These small stores tend to charge higher prices than their larger counterparts. For example, in Newark, New Jersey, prices at small grocery stores were as much as 38% higher than at suburban supermarkets (Bremner, 1990).

There are many reasons for the higher prices charged by small retailers. As mentioned earlier, the absence of a large retail outlet leaves the remaining small-store merchants with less competition and less incentive to maintain competitive prices. Large retail outlets generally have more product variety and the ability to charge lower prices. In addition, the higher costs associated with inner-city locations apply to small as well as to large merchants. Furthermore, small stores do not enjoy the economies of scale of larger operations. This means fixed costs are a larger part of the per unit cost paid by customers, and small stores must buy in smaller quantities and face higher wholesale costs, which are passed on to the consumer. Not all price differences are justified by cost differentials, however. Prices at some local stores in poor neighborhoods have been observed to increase the day that welfare checks are received (Bremner, 1990).

At the same time, small neighborhood stores may offer benefits to poor local residents that they cannot get from multistore outlets. Small grocery stores sometimes serve as an informal source of credit, allowing customers to delay payment until a check arrives. For poor consumers, this benefit may outweigh the lower costs of buying groceries from chain supermarkets.

SUMMARY

In summary, one requirement for price discrimination, market isolation, is satisfied in the retail markets of poor communities. The other, lower price sensitivity of poor consumers, depends on the product and would seem to limit the effectiveness of price discrimination. The extent to which poor people hire transportation to shop for food outside their neighborhoods is an example of how price discrimination is limited by poor consumers. But substantial evidence exists to support the hypothesis that the poor not only pay higher direct prices for products but also face nonpecuniary charges.

To the extent that the poor are geographically segregated and predominantly poor areas have fewer retail establishments, businesses face less competitive pressure, allowing them to charge higher prices to a captive market. This means that consumers pay more when they shop locally in neighborhoods with few outlets. To pay prices comparable to those in neighborhoods with more outlets, consumers must expend time, effort, and money in travel. Both of these options lead to higher prices for people least able to afford them—those who live in low-income neighborhoods.

RETAIL BUSINESSES IN INNER CITIES

The neighborhood has a large number of vacant homes, some burnt-out buildings, a lot more liquor stores, and fewer supermarkets than one would expect to see, and many people are on the streets during the day when you would expect them to be at work. You are a retailer looking for a site for a new outlet. Are you willing to consider such a neighborhood? What would consumers feel about a retail store located in that setting? Surely they see it as unattractive, unsafe, and unlikely to have the goods they want and need.

Between 1970 and 1988, Los Angeles, Chicago, Brooklyn, and Manhattan lost almost 40% of their population. This flight from the city was accompanied by an even greater decline in the number of retail outlets in the city. Almost one half of the supermarkets in the three largest U.S. cities closed during the period. Why did the retail stores leave? Which ones now serve the needs of poor consumers in inner-city neighborhoods?

In addition to decreases in market size, owners of fleeing retail outlets complained of high labor costs, high insurance premiums, high levels of stock loss, higher rents, lower sales volume, and lower profits as causes for their out-migration from the inner city. Another reason for fleeing was the diminished purchasing power of the remaining population. Wilson (1987) has argued that the people who left cities were those with above-average incomes.

The number of retail outlets in an area is a function of both the demand for goods and services and the costs of doing business there. Declines in inner-city population are tantamount to decreases in demand for local merchants. When population decreases were accompanied by falling average purchasing power, as hypothesized by Wilson (1987) and empirically verified by Danziger and Gottschalk (1987), demand would have fallen precipitously in the inner city during the 1960s and 1970s.

All else being equal, a decrease in demand should lead to increased local competition among retailers in the short run. Retailers would lower prices and take lower profit margins. In the long run, the effects are not as beneficial, as the lower profit margins would cause retail outlets to exit the market. From a theoretical perspective, decreases in demand do not lead to higher prices. In reality, however, retailers' responses to decreases in demand for goods and services may overcompensate for the decrease in demand and prices may increase. Supermarkets serve as a case in point.

The exit of one supermarket from a neighborhood because of lower profitability may more than compensate for an initial decrease in demand. In this case, the decrease in demand and the resulting decrease in the amount of product being supplied (the exit of one supermarket) leads to less competition among the remaining merchants for the remaining demand. Consequently, the decrease in demand does *not* lead to the anticipated decrease in prices, but rather its opposite, higher prices, as the result of lower levels of effective market competition.

Another factor that influences the number of retail outlets in an area and the prices they charge concerns the costs of conducting business. Substantial evidence documents the higher costs of doing business in an inner city. Consider the exit of a supermarket from a neighborhood because of lower profitability. Its lower profitability may be partially due to additional operations costs in urban areas. These include additional payroll costs for security, expenses associated with greater regulation from local governmental agencies, and a less-educated labor force that needs more training and supervision. All of these operational factors act to increase prices. Either these cost increases are passed on to consumers or businesses experience decreases in profitability (Hammel, 1991; Porter, 1995).

Multioutlet supermarkets that consider opening or expanding an outlet in a poor neighborhood face additional barriers. Supermarket chains find it profitable to open large outlets, but it is difficult to find adequately sized sites in inner-city poor neighborhoods due to fragmentation of ownership. Another barrier is in the form of zoning and permit requirements. In New

York City, many potential sites are limited because of zoning laws (Bremner, 1990). For example, Pathmark Supermarkets negotiated to locate a store in the East Harlem section of New York City. After 4 years, the store obtained the approval of the Manhattan Borough Council, but it is still blocked by political, community, and other regulatory barriers (Pulley, 1995; Traub, 1995).

Finally, due to the historical abandonment of inner-city areas by retail outlets, there is a measure of distrust between community organizations and business establishments. Community organizations frequently demand land set asides or special training programs as evidence of a firm's commitment to the community. These programs, no matter how well intended, reduce the profitability of inner-city operations and consequently make the establishment or reestablishment of businesses in the inner city less likely to occur. All of these factors not only contributed to the initial flight from urban markets but remain as potential barriers to current expansion of retail outlets in the inner city.

HOW TO SUCCEED IN INNER-CITY NEIGHBORHOODS

Not only is it possible to run a successful large business in an inner-city neighborhood, but the successful store offers several key advantages over a smaller counterpart. A larger store typically offers lower prices than smaller stores in the neighborhood, as well as a clean, secure environment, satisfying the needs of local customers. For example, a Pathmark supermarket that recently opened in an enterprise zone in Newark claims it is successful because it offers products preferred by customers and is clean, well lit, and secure.

The secret of success for retailers in poor neighborhoods includes several elements. Most important is for retail businesses to be convinced that locating in poor neighborhoods can be profitable. Porter (1995) argues that businesses will not be attracted to inner-city neighborhoods by philanthropic motives, by governmental or privately based incentives, by government mandates, or even by the development of small businesses supported by community organizations. Rather, he argues that inner-city neighborhoods must be revitalized by the private sector integrating the inner city into the regional economy. Local businesses, he suggests, should not only serve the local community but seek to "export" their goods and services. For example, an inner-city music store with expertise in Hispanic music should capitalize on this expertise by offering the specialty in other areas of the city or in other cities with a large percentage of Hispanic residents.

Porter (1995) points out that inner cities offer several advantages to businesses. Of particular interest to retailers are that

- Their high and growing population density can ensure high business volume despite a low per capita income
- The current lack of competition for much of retailing offers an advantage to early entrants
- The large labor pool for service workers in retailing promises selection of qualified employees

In addition to these advantages, the saturation of retailing in suburban areas makes inner-city areas attractive as a new retailing frontier (Miller, 1994).

Another element to retailer success in poor neighborhoods is for consumers to perceive that shopping near and in the retail store is secure. A Boston supermarket in a Hispanic neighborhood that specializes in Hispanic packaged goods and produce finds it has little problem with security, either in or outside the store. The Boston store attributes its good security record to drawing enough foot traffic to the store location that would-be thieves are deterred both from the supermarket and nearby stores (ICIC Leadership Conference, personal communication, April 21, 1995). This critical mass of foot traffic can be developed by locating a number of retail outlets in one location, by including a high-traffic retail outlet that draws customers to a retail outlet complex, by making stores and surrounding areas attractive, or by providing highly visible security protection. How to provide security is not always obvious. One inner-city business planted bushes in a vacant lot across the street from its location in an effort to make the location attractive. It was found, however, that potential customers were made even more fearful because they were afraid muggers would hide in the bushes (Grzywinwki, 1991).

A third element to retail success in poor neighborhoods is building links to the local community and becoming part of that community. The Hispanic supermarket in Boston makes special efforts to develop a friendly relationship with its customers by, for example, hanging flags of the nations from which its customers immigrated and playing music from those nations in the store (ICIC Leadership Conference, personal communication, April

21, 1995). The Pathmark supermarket in Newark maintains strong ties with the local community, for example, by holding health screening tests on its premises, sponsoring an annual festival, and offering a shuttle service to the bus. Good community relations can be accomplished most easily by businesses run by people who live in the community, by employing local residents, and by making strong efforts to train employees and instill in them loyalty to the business. It also can be accomplished by offering services to the community, participation by the business in community affairs, and creating a friendly store image in the minds of consumers.

A fourth element is to provide for the specific needs of local consumers. This can take various forms. It may mean offering foods, clothing, books, or music that appeal to the local population or different colors or sizes, no-frills goods, or quality goods at a fair price.

Despite formidable barriers, some large supermarket chains are showing renewed interest in opening outlets in low-income neighborhoods. Stop & Shop recently opened its first chain supermarket in downtown Boston in 20 years, and other supermarket chains have similar plans (Diesenhouse, 1993). Supermarkets are following suit in other cities, such as Houston, Los Angeles, Cleveland, and Chicago.

In addition, other organizations are helping businesses locate in inner cities. The Food Marketing Institute is identifying potential sites for supermarkets in inner cities ("Shops in Inner Cities," 1992). A consortium of eight firms, a pension fund, and a foundation have established an equity fund to support shopping centers in poor neighborhoods (Chetwynd, 1994). A nonprofit organization, the Initiative for a Competitive Inner City, helps businesses enter or grow in inner cities by facilitating consulting by teams of supervised business school students.

SUMMARY

Businesses tend to locate in areas where they will make the most profit, areas of high demand and low costs of doing business. Compared to suburban areas, inner-city neighborhoods may be less attractive because of the higher costs of doing business and lower purchasing power of the community. In general, inner-city neighborhoods are less able to support as many retail establishments as a wealthier community.

There are several reasons to encourage the establishment of businesses, particularly large ones, in poor areas. Residents of those areas face higher prices due to fewer large retail outlets and higher costs of conducting business. Although per capita income is low in poor neighborhoods, the population density can result in a profitable business for a large retailer (Porter, 1995). Retailers in poor neighborhoods can succeed by taking into account their consumers' needs and preferences. Finally, satiation by retailers of more profitable neighborhoods leads them to seek additional sources of growth, and poor neighborhoods are excellent candidates for those growth sources.

SHOPPING IN CHICAGO'S
POOR NEIGHBORHOODS

Unless you have lived in a poor neighborhood, it is difficult to envision the enormity of problems faced by poor consumers seeking goods and services. To attempt to bring this experience to the reader, in this section we illustrate the extent to which access to products is limited, using one city, Chicago, as a case history. We describe and examine the distribution of retail outlets in the city of Chicago to identify differences in the availability of consumer goods and services for poor and nonpoor consumers. Although Chicago may differ in many ways from other urban areas, it also reflects trends in other urban centers. A recent survey of supermarkets in different income areas of 21 urban centers across the nation found that the pattern in Chicago reflected that of the nation and of 12 other urban centers in the sample (Cotterill & Franklin, 1995).

Ideally, such an analysis would be based on the alternative retail outlets available to individual families that differ in their income levels. For example, one might identify the number of retail outlets within a specified distance of a family's residence to calculate the amount of competition for the family's consumption dollars. There are two problems with such an approach. Most important, for confidentiality reasons data are not available reporting family incomes with household addresses. Second, it is difficult to specify the marketplace for any given family. For example, families with an automobile or reliable public transportation would have access to a larger geographic area and consequently to more stores. Due to these problems, we rely on zip code areas as the basic unit of analysis. Zip codes, like any predefined geographic boundary, do not capture true market boundaries, but they do allow for a spatial analysis of the distribution of retail outlets and their correlation with consumer income and well-being.

The data for the analysis are derived from two independent sources. The Economic Census of the United States reports the number of retail outlets in each zip code area by category of primary sales (type of store) as well as by number of employees (U.S. Bureau of the Census, 1990). The number of employees is used as a surrogate measure of the size of the retail establishment. *The Sourcebook of Zip Code Demographics* (CACI Marketing Systems, 1994) provides data on a variety of household characteristics by zip code. By merging these two files, we are able to identify poor areas and document the number of different types and sizes of retail establishments in poor and nonpoor areas. Note that this analysis is limited to the *number* of retail stores of different types and sizes and does not consider the quality of the product or the quality of the shopping experience. It often has been observed that stores in poor areas carry a limited variety of products, carry outdated or shelf-worn products, and may not be as clean as stores in more affluent areas (e.g., Zimmerman & Fields, 1995).

DEFINING POOR AREAS

The first step is defining poor areas. As discussed in Chapter 4, the poorest members of urban areas, the underclass, live in neighborhoods with a variety of problems. These problems include low income, low level of education, low participation in the labor force, and high unemployment. This analysis defines a zip code area as poor on the basis of the distribution of four characteristics that reflect these problems. A zip code area is defined as poor if it meets all four of the following criteria: (a) The poverty rate is in the highest 25%, (b) the high school graduation rate is in the bottom 25%, (c) the labor force participation rate is in the bottom 25%, and (d) the unemployment rate is in the top 25%.

The cutoff values for inclusion as a poor zip code area are a poverty rate greater than 28%, a high school graduation rate less than 56%, a labor force participation rate lower than 60%, and an unemployment rate less than 14.6%. These criteria yield 7 poverty areas out of 54 zip code areas, or 13% of all Chicago zip code areas. Table 8.1 summarizes these characteristics for all zip code areas in poor and nonpoor areas. This is a stringent definition of poor areas. For example, it excludes six zip code areas with poverty rates greater than 28% and five zip code areas with less than 56% high school graduation. In general, it excludes zip code areas in transition

TABLE 8.1 Demographic Summary by Zip Code

	Poor Zip Codes	Nonpoor Zip Codes	All Zip Codes
Median household income	$16,673	$33,350	$31,188
Number of households	22,178	21,472	21,564
Poverty rate	42.0%	14.5%	18.1%
Percentage high school graduates	47.8	71.2	68.2
Percentage in labor force	51.4	65.2	63.4
Unemployment rate	24.6%	9.0%	11.0%

from more to less affluent or vice versa. The advantage of this stringent definition of poor areas is that it allows us to plainly observe differences in the distribution of retail establishments in poor and nonpoor areas.

There are distinct differences between poor and nonpoor areas. Poverty rates and the level of unemployment are significantly higher in poor areas than in nonpoor areas, and the percentage of the population with high school degrees and participating in the labor force is lower in poor areas. In terms of demographic characteristics not used to define poor and nonpoor areas, poor areas, have median household incomes approximately one half the size of nonpoor areas, and the housing stock in these areas is predominantly older multiunit housing occupied by renters. Most important, population density across zip codes is similar. This means that aggregate purchasing power differences between poor and nonpoor zip code areas are nearly identical to the differences in median household income.

Geographically, the seven zip codes that satisfy the definition of poor areas form a contiguous ring sector around the central business district of the city to the south and west.[6] This pattern is consistent with other geodemographic descriptions of Chicago (e.g., Metro Chicago Information Center, 1994). Figures 8.1 through 8.3 show the location of these poverty areas in the city of Chicago and report demographic statistics relative to their poverty status.

Figure 8.1 shows that the seven poverty areas all have the lowest levels of aggregate household income in the sample. Figure 8.2 highlights the low levels of labor force participation in these areas relative to other zip code areas. Perhaps most striking is the information conveyed in Figure 8.3 reporting the percentage of the housing stock that is vacant. Although a few nonpoverty zip code areas have vacancy rates similar to those of the

(text continues on page 145)

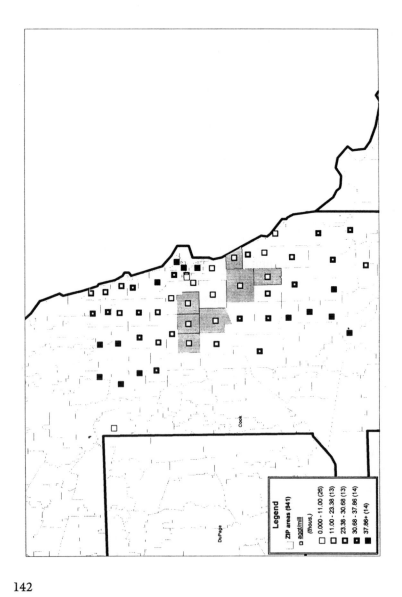

Figure 8.1. Chicago Aggregate

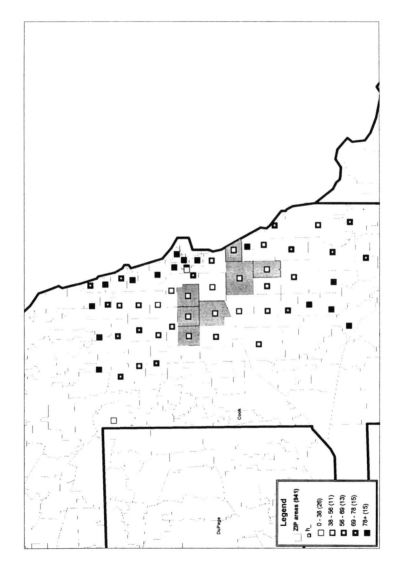

Legend

ZIP areas (941)

□ h_

□ 0 - 38 (26)
□ 38 - 56 (11)
□ 56 - 69 (13)
■ 69 - 78 (15)
■ 78+ (15)

Cook

DuPage

Figure 8.2. Chicago Percentage in Labor Force

143

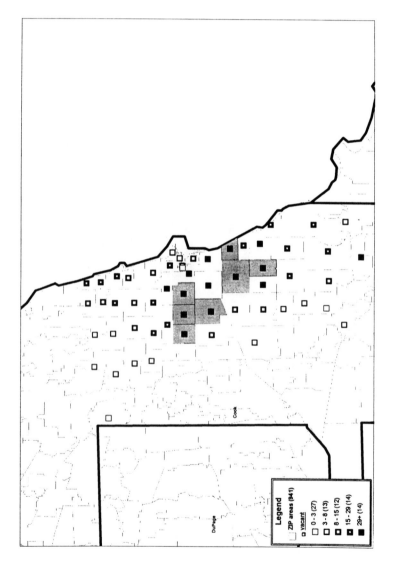

Legend
ZIP areas (941)
vacant
□ 0 - 3 (27)
□ 3 - 8 (13)
▣ 8 - 15 (12)
▣ 15 - 29 (14)
■ 29+ (14)

DuPage

Cook

Figure 8.3. Chicago Vacant Housing

poverty areas, these zip code areas are in fact adjacent to the poverty areas. In brief, Figures 8.1 through 8.3 attest to the severity of the poverty in the poor zip code areas and illustrate the geographic concentration of poverty in the city of Chicago.

DISTRIBUTION OF RETAIL ESTABLISHMENTS

The Census of Retail Trade reports statistics on retail businesses as categorized in the Standard Industrial Classification (SIC) Manual. Of the several hundred distinct types of businesses in the classification, we selected five types of establishments for analysis. In this section, we examine the distribution of all retail establishments and of grocery stores, apparel stores, drinking establishments, liquor stores, and drugstores with data derived from the Census of Retail Trade. In addition, we collected data from the Prophone 1995 CD-ROM telephone database on the number of banks in each Chicago zip code area.

Grocery stores were chosen for analysis due to the large portion of total expenditures that food purchases constitute of the average poor family's budget. Drugstores were chosen to quantify the ability of consumers in poor versus nonpoor areas to satisfy their needs for personal and health care goods. Banks were examined to determine the distribution of financial services in poor areas. Finally, liquor and drinking establishments were analyzed to test the perception that poor areas have more than their share of such "sin" outlets.

Poor areas not only have fewer general retail outlets than nonpoor areas, the retail outlets in poor areas are also smaller. Table 8.2 compares the distribution of different types and sizes of retail outlets in poor and nonpoor zip code areas.[7] Poor areas have a smaller number of general retail outlets than nonpoor areas. On average, poor zip code areas contain a total of 164.6 retail outlets compared to 247.0 stores in nonpoor areas and 236.3 stores per zip code area citywide. The difference between the poor and the nonpoor zip code areas in the total number of retail stores is significant ($t(52) = 1.71, p = .09$). Poor areas have more liquor stores and fewer banks, but there is no statistically significant difference between the number of grocery, apparel, drinking establishments, or drugstores. Although poor areas have a greater number of liquor stores ($t(20) = 4.44$, $p = .000$), they have significantly fewer drinking establishments ($t(12) = 2.62, p =. 01$). Most important, poor zip code areas have less than one half the average number of banking outlets than nonpoor areas.

TABLE 8.2 Average Number of Outlets per Zip Code Area

Establishment Type	Poor Zip Codes	Nonpoor Zip Codes	All Zip Codes
All retail (1)	164.6	247.0***	236.3
All grocery (1)	20.9	16.2	11.0
Grocery 1 to 9 employees (1)	16.9***	10.1	11.0
Grocery 10 or more employees (2)	4.0	6.1***	5.8
Supermarkets (2)	1.1	2.4***	2.2
Apparel (2)	16.7	23.5	22.7
Drinking establishments (2)	7.1	14.6***	13.6
All liquor (2)	11.3***	7.2	7.8
Liquor 1 to 9 employees (2)	10.4***	6.2	6.7
Liquor 10 or more employees (1)	0.9	1.0	0.9
All drug (2)	10.3	10.9	10.9
Drug 1 to 4 employees (2)	7.7***	4.1	4.5
Drug 5 or more employees (1)	2.6	6.9***	6.3
All banks (1)	2.3	5.0**	4.7

NOTE: (1) Equal variance; (2) Unequal variance.
$* p < .10; ** p < .05; *** p < .01.$

There are more retail establishments in poor areas, but they are typically small stores. Poor areas have more grocery stores with fewer than 10 employees. They also have fewer than one half the number of supermarkets (identified as stores with 50 or more employees). Nonpoor areas report an average of 2.4 supermarkets and the citywide average is 2.2, but poor areas only have 1.1 supermarkets. The difference between the number of supermarkets in poor and nonpoor areas is significant ($t(16) = 2.74, p = .01$). The same holds true for drugstores. Although the total number of drugstores is not significantly different between poor and nonpoor areas, poor areas have fewer drugstores with more than four employees ($t(52) = 2.93, p < .000$) and more drugstores with one to four employees ($t(13) = 4.41, p < .000$).

Figures 8.4 and 8.5 highlight the distribution of grocery stores across the city of Chicago. Small groceries (those with fewer than five full-time equivalent employees) are distributed unevenly throughout the city. The poor zip code areas can clearly be seen to have more than the average number, however, with four of seven of the poverty areas falling into the top 19 zip code areas in total number of small groceries. Supermarkets are another story. Five of the six poverty zip code areas contain one or fewer supermarkets, and the remaining poverty zip code area contains three supermarkets. This is far fewer, on average, than for the balance of zip code areas in the city.

(text continues on page 151)

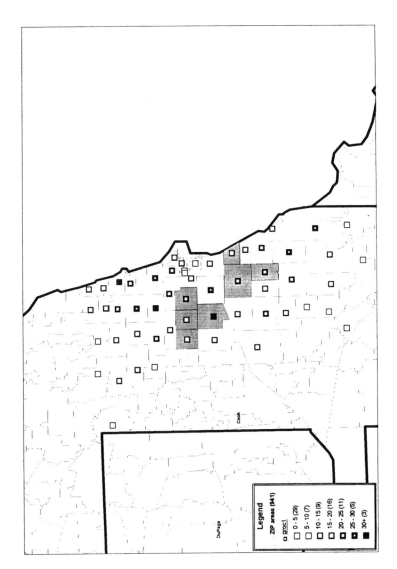

Figure 8.4. Chicago Small Groceries

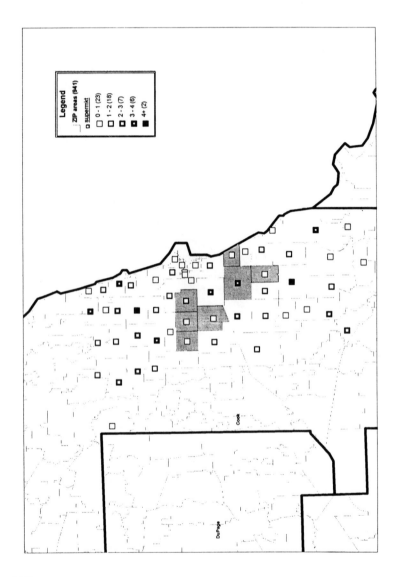

Figure 8.5. Chicago Supermarkets

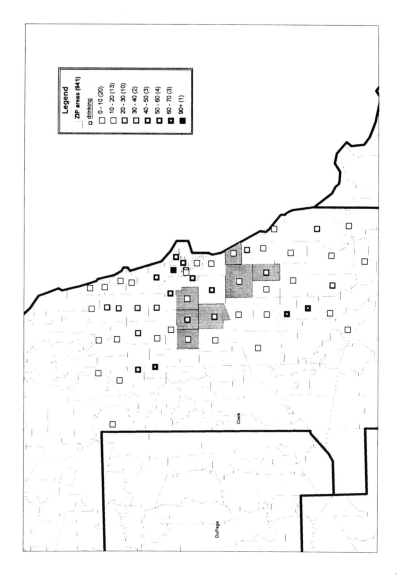

Figure 8.6. Chicago Drinking Establishments

149

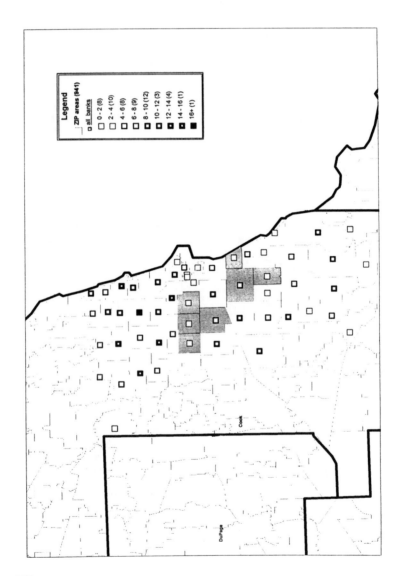

Figure 8.7. Chicago Banks

150

Figure 8.6 maps the distribution of taverns and drinking establishments across the city. Although poverty areas have, on average, fewer such establishments, they are not strikingly different from the typical zip code area in this regard. Rather, a handful of nonpoor zip code areas hold the majority of drinking establishments in the city of Chicago. Figure 8.7 shows the clear difference in the geographic distribution of banks between poverty and nonpoverty zip codes. All but one of the poverty zip code areas have two or fewer banks, compared to an average of five banks per zip code area in the nonpoor areas.

As discussed earlier in this chapter, the impact of the number of retail outlets is only one influence on prices charged for comparable products in poor areas relative to nonpoor areas. The literature on spatial economics argues that the effect of additional retail outlets on market prices is a function of store density and the relative role of transportation costs. Some authors have argued that with low store density and high transportation costs the entrance of an additional competitor may even increase market prices (Capozza & Van Order, 1978)—consumers may be willing to pay for easier accessibility and less transportation time. Once distance from existing merchants is explicitly controlled for, the price effect of an additional supermarket actually decreases prices (Walden, 1991).

Thus, all else being equal, a greater number of merchants in the poor areas should lead to greater price competition. Nonetheless, the smaller scale of the stores (e.g., fewer supermarkets and large drugstores) in poor areas implies higher costs that would be expected to be passed on to residents of the poor areas. An increase in the number of larger retail outlets would undoubtedly benefit the poor communities. Earlier, we suggested various barriers that result in a scarcity of retailers in poor areas; these data allow a test of one reason why larger retail outlets are scarce.

That reason may be that big businesses decide on the location of outlet sites primarily on the basis of an area's purchasing power. If purchasing power does not differ between poor and nonpoor areas, big businesses may not see any justification for locating more outlets in poor areas. We test this hypothesis by using aggregate income in each zip code area as a surrogate for that zip code area's purchasing power.

The hypothesis is supported for supermarkets and banks. Supermarkets and banks may maintain the number of outlets in poor areas commensurate with their purchasing power. This ratio of number of outlets to purchasing power is constant for poor and nonpoor zip code areas. When the

TABLE 8.3 Average Number of Outlets per Million Dollars of Aggregate Income

Establishment Type	Poor Zip Codes	Nonpoor Zip Codes	All Zip Codes
All retail (1)	0.465	0.409	0.417
All grocery (1)	0.060***	0.026	0.030
Grocery 1 to 9 employees (1)	0.048***	0.016	0.020
Grocery 10 or more employees (1)	0.011	0.010	0.010
Supermarkets (1)	0.003	0.003	0.003
Apparel (1)	0.049	0.043	0.043
Drinking establishments (1)	0.018	0.022	0.022
All liquor (2)	0.035***	0.011	0.015
Liquor 1 to 9 employees (2)	0.032***	0.010	0.013
Liquor 10 or more employees (1)	0.003	0.002	0.002
All drug (2)	0.031***	0.017	0.019
Drug 1 to 5 employees (2)	0.024***	0.007	0.009
Drug 5 or more employees (1)	0.007	0.010*	0.010
All banks (2)	0.005	0.008	0.007

NOTE: (1) Equal variance; (2) Unequal variance.
* $p < .10$; ** $p < .05$; *** $p < .01$.

purchasing power in a zip code area is controlled for, there is no statistically significant difference between the number of outlets in poor and nonpoor areas (see Table 8.3). Poor and nonpoor areas have 0.003 supermarkets per million dollars of purchasing power. Although poor areas have 0.005 banks per million dollars of purchasing power versus 0.008 for nonpoor areas, the difference in number of banking outlets between areas is only significant at the 10% level.

The hypothesis that big businesses decide on the locations of outlet sites primarily on the basis of the area's purchasing power does not explain the scarcity of outlets of large drugstore chains or the profusion of liquor stores in poor zip code areas. Larger drugstores are still underrepresented in poor areas even after controlling for purchasing power—0.007 to 0.010 large drugstores per million dollars of purchasing power ($p < .01$). In addition, all liquor stores are overrepresented in poor areas after controlling for purchasing power—0.035 liquor stores per million dollars of purchasing power in poor versus 0.011 in nonpoor areas ($p < .01$).

An implication of this analysis is that big businesses that do not locate outlet sites in poor neighborhoods solely because of aggregate area purchasing power must become aware of the other influences on the success of a business in the poor inner city. As discussed in Chapters 3 and

4, income alone is not a good indicator of the amount purchased and consumed by the poor. If the income surrogate for purchasing power used in this analysis could be adjusted for other financial resources, it is likely that poor areas would indeed show a disadvantage compared to nonpoor areas. Other influences than purchasing power (or demand) on successful ventures in poor neighborhoods were discussed earlier in this chapter.

From the point of view of the poor consumer, fewer retail outlets mean higher prices, less variety of product and less choice, and an unsatisfactory shopping experience. They also mean that getting to and from the stores is difficult. When retail outlets are far from where one lives and transportation is either unavailable or too expensive, the shopper buys less because less can be carried home.

SUMMARY

Retailers offer some rational reasons for leaving or not entering poor communities. Marketers may have legitimate business reasons for price differentials that do not favor low-income consumers. Grocery store chains argue that stores in low-income neighborhoods have higher overhead costs due to pilferage and the need to supply more security. Banks argue that there are higher costs to operating branches in poor neighborhoods because, for example, many customers maintain minimal balances and carry out a large number of small-value transactions. In sum, for businesses the cost of doing business with poor consumers is often perceived to be higher than with more affluent consumers. Nevertheless, there are opportunities for successful retail businesses in poor areas today.

There are both good business reasons and good ethical reasons for abolishing price discrimination against poor consumers. Many businesses are insufficiently aware that there is profit to be gained by attracting poor consumers to a brand or to a retail outlet. Poor consumers are well aware of the higher prices and lower values offered to them and are entitled to a more balanced exchange. Many businesses, both retail and manufacturing, also seem to use short-term strategies in their customer relationships, not recognizing that today's poor are likely to be tomorrow's affluent customer.

In addition, it is not clear that the best ethical solution to higher costs of doing business with the poor is to make poor consumers bear the entire cost of this incremental business expense. An alternative policy for firms with multiple outlets, such as chain food stores or large banks, would be to spread the costs of doing business across all consumers. Just as the more affluent customers benefit from quantity savings permissible because of the presence of lower-income consumers, so should they be obligated to cover the costs of business expenses. Smaller retailers can and have formed buying cooperatives to lower their product costs.

NOTES

1. Reprinted with permission from the *Miami Sun-Sentinel,* Fort Lauderdale, Florida.

2. Reprinted by permission of the *Wall Street Journal.* Copyright © 1993 by the Dow Jones & Company, Inc. All rights reserved worldwide.

3. Section 2 of the Clayton Act, enacted in 1914 (and amended by the Robinson-Patman Act of 1936), states:

> It shall be unlawful for any person engaged in commerce, in the course of such commerce, either directly or indirectly, to discriminate in price between different purchasers of commodities of like grade and quality . . . where the effect of such discrimination may be to substantially lessen competition or tend to create a monopoly in any line of commerce, or to injure, destroy, or prevent competition.

4. There are actually three different types of price discrimination, depending on whether discrimination affects competition among sellers, buyers, or customers of buyers (Ortmeyer, 1993). The most common form of price discrimination encountered is the last, and that form is assumed in the discussion.

5. The assumption that firms act to maximize profits leads to certain actions. One simple prediction of profit-maximizing behavior is that markup (the difference between marginal cost of production and price) is inversely related to price elasticity of demand. For example, airlines recognize that business travelers are less sensitive to the price of airfare than are leisure travelers, and airfare pricing reflects this difference. Airlines regularly discount airfares planned well in advance to attract leisure travelers and charge substantially higher prices for business travel, which is typically booked near the date of travel.

6. Lake Michigan forms a natural boundary to the east of the central business district, and the affluent Lincoln Park area borders the north end.

7. Statistical tests for comparisons of means assumed either equal or unequal variance based on the results of an F-test for equal variances. When variances were found to be unequal based on the result of the F-test, a heteroscedastistic t-test was performed and the degrees of freedom are then a function of the size of the estimated standard errors.

9

Conclusions and Implications:
Extending the Theory
of Marketing Exchange

The poor shall never cease out of the land.

—Numbers 15:11

Then I began to think that it is very true which is commonly said,
that the one half of the world knoweth not how the other half liveth.

—Rabelais (1963, p. 307)

A s the preceding quotes eloquently state, it seems inevitable that the
poor are a permanent fixture of society. Nonetheless, the plight of
the poor in their roles as consumers can clearly be improved through
changes in business and public attitudes and in government action. In this
book, we have identified areas in which poor consumers face obstacles to
their well-being.

Poor consumers are quite diverse. Each different segment—single mothers
and their children, mentally or physically disabled people, the elderly, the
temporarily poor, the long-term poor, urban dwellers, rural dwellers, and
suburban dwellers—has different needs and requires different kinds of attention from marketers and society. As members of society, marketers share the

attitudes about poverty and welfare held in our society and are likely to hold inaccurate stereotypes of poor people. For marketers, however, these inaccurate stereotypes can lead to inappropriate business decisions.

Poor consumers clearly suffer inequities in marketing exchanges that reach beyond their limited incomes. Although low income may explain their inability to get enough food or the right kinds of food, their choice also may be limited to outdated food packages at higher prices. In addition, poor consumers typically spend proportionately more of their financial resources for housing and frequently live in substandard housing. They often must rely on public transportation with all its shortcomings. They pay more for managing their finances and often must travel farther than the more affluent for their financial transactions.

Poor consumers undoubtedly suffer in marketing exchanges with unethical businesspeople, and poor people are probably just as likely to be the victims of disregard by consumer businesses. They are commonly ignored by businesses that do not consider their needs as a separate market segment or shunned as a risky or unprofitable market segment. In all, the application of standard marketing concepts to poor consumers results in an imbalance of a marketing exchange in favor of business.

In the preceding chapters, we have argued that although poor consumers differ from the nonpoor population in many respects, perceptions of them by the general public are frequently incorrect. For example, in Chapter 5 we noted the divergence between the actual consumption patterns of poor consumers and public perceptions of how the poor spend their money for food. In general, poor consumers appear to live carefully within their limited means and take steps to get the best value for their dollars. They do not splurge on fast food, snacks, convenient but expensive foods, or liquor. On the other hand, poor consumers may be more limited than more affluent consumers in the variety of products they can buy and in the suitability of products for their needs.

We also have explored some characteristics of marketing exchanges particular to poor consumers. In Chapter 8, we examined price differentials charged to poor consumers and characteristics of the marketplace in predominantly poor areas. In terms of paying higher prices, those of the poor who have few alternatives (such as urban poor who live in poor neighborhoods) are indeed vulnerable to abuses in the marketplace. They pay higher prices at several different types of retail stores, for fees to manage their finances, and for some other products and services.

In terms of retail outlets to shop at, poor consumers also are limited by market structure. There are fewer stores that offer value—quality products at fair prices—in their neighborhoods than in more affluent neighborhoods. We did not discuss susceptibility of poor consumers to direct sales approaches and specific sales tactics, primarily because little evidence is available for evaluation. One can speculate that in a face-to-face encounter with a sales-person, the nontangible aspects of a marketing exchange would play a particularly important role. For example, the value a poor customer derives from an exchange will be enhanced by the positive emotional benefits from dealing with a friendly salesperson who, for example, sweet-talks to boost the customer's self-esteem. This should be particularly true for poor consumers who are well aware that the actual products they can afford to buy may have lower value because they include interest payments for paying on time. One reason poor consumers enter into the exchange and agree to pay more for less value may have to do with the nontangible aspects of the exchange, the positive experience of the sale itself.

In terms of marketing communications directed to poor consumers, we indicated in Chapter 7 that with a few well-publicized exceptions such as billboards for tobacco and alcohol, there do not appear to be blatant abuses of advertising or other marketing communications directed to poor consumers. Poor consumers may be ignored by some media used for marketing communications, but the products advertised in places they are likely to be exposed to that advertising are for the most part products of use to them. We have little empirical evidence dealing with poor consum-ers' abilities to cope with marketing communications, however, so their vulnerability to advertising and promotions is still an open question.

In sum, the poor are more vulnerable as consumers in some aspects of their marketing exchanges than in others. The overriding questions are whether the marketplace can adequately serve the poor consumer, how much government intervention in market exchanges is necessary to guar-antee poor consumers sufficient protection in the marketplace, and how much social services can help balance the exchange. To the extent they are vulnerable, should poor consumers be protected? If so, by whom and how? What is the role of paternalism by regulators, social service provid-ers, and society in putting the exchange between poor consumers and other parties in better balance? These are politically loaded questions.

Intervention by social service providers, government, or other seg-ments of society in situations in which poor consumers are vulnerable must depend on the reasons for the vulnerabilities and on the effects of the vulnerabilities on the poor consumers. To the extent that the basis for a vulnerability of poor consumers is market structure, there is a greater call for intervention. Governmental regulation of the marketplace would seem to be a primary solution. For example, the government can reduce the need for the poor to use currency exchanges that charge a usurious rate by using debit cards to provide welfare financial aid (discussed later in this chapter). To the extent that the basis for the vulnerability of poor consumers is their own behavior or characteristics, then a different type of intervention is called for. This type of intervention could be education, encouragement to take responsibility for their own behavior, and incentives to help poor consumers to better cope with marketing exchanges— for example, helping poor consumers to form small cooperative buying groups to save money (a suggestion discussed in more detail in a later section).

All problems of poor consumers cannot be solved at one time. Aspects of marketing exchanges that prey on the vulnerabilities of poor consumers must be prioritized. Those that cause the most harm to poor consumers are clearly the ones that must receive attention first. Vulnerabilities can be prioritized by (a) those that place the poor consumer in harm; (b) those that are the result of illegal actions by other parties to an exchange; (c) those that result in inequitable prices; and (d) those that result in inequitable demands on time and effort, resulting in inconvenience. Alternatively, vulnerabilities of poor consumers could be prioritized according to Maslow's (1970) hierarchy of needs: (a) those that affect sustenance, such as food and housing; (b) those that affect physical safety; (c) those that affect relationships with other people and institutions in society; (d) those that affect esteem needs; and (e) those that allow one to fulfill one's best capabilities.

A REVISED THEORY OF MARKETING EXCHANGE WITH POOR CONSUMERS

To organize our thoughts about solutions to the problems of poor consumers, we present a revised theory of marketing exchange, extended from Bagozzi's (1975) model. Our model is intended as a more accurate description of exchanges between marketers and poor consumers. In

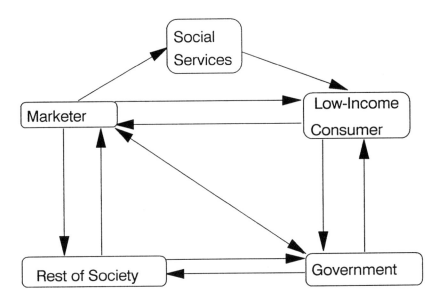

Figure 9.1. Revised Marketing Exchange Model

addition to marketers and poor consumers, the revised model includes government, the public, and social service agencies as parties to the exchange. We identify paths in the exchange and illustrate them with examples.

The traditional and simplest view of exchange is between two parties, most often a buyer and a seller. Recall that, as Bagozzi (1975) noted, social marketing exchange transactions often include more than one party (see Chapter 2). Figure 9.1 shows a revised marketing exchange model that includes poor consumers and for-profit marketers. Society pays taxes to government and makes donations to social service agencies; government provides welfare and social agencies provide services to poor people. As Bagozzi points out, by providing welfare and services to poor people, government and social services give the rest of society protection against other means that poor people could use to obtain what they need (such as taking it). Government and social services offer reassurance that, if needed, a safety net is available for people without the means to enter the exchange on their own. In addition, government can regulate marketers and reduce marketer risks in transactions with poor consumers. The more

TABLE 9.1 Five Public and Social Policy Implications to Equalize the Balance
            in Marketing Exchanges With Poor Consumers

Implication	Ethical Foundation
1. Increase what poor consumers have to exchange	Equity
2. Increase the exchange power of poor consumers	Commitment and Equity
3. Decrease the exchange power of marketer	Equity
4. Alter what marketers have to exchange	Equity
5. Reduce perceived marketer risk	Responsibility and Trust

affluent sectors of society can, by some of their purchases, enable marketers
to carry out "social marketing," which can be used to benefit poor directly.
For example, in buying products from firms such as Ben & Jerry's Ice
Cream, consumers know that a portion of the profits will be donated to
charitable causes. Nevertheless, the exchange between marketer and poor
consumer may be unbalanced unless the paths among the components of
the model are used to find ways to make this exchange more equitable.

PUBLIC AND SOCIAL POLICY IMPLICATIONS: GENERAL

One goal pursued here is to find ways to enhance the ethical foundations of exchange for parties to marketing exchanges that include poor
consumers. Table 9.1 shows five approaches to reducing the imbalance in
exchanges between marketers and poor consumers and the ethical foundation of exchange these approaches are likely to increase.

One approach is for regulators to *increase what poor consumers have to
exchange.* This approach has been used primarily by government welfare,
for example, with the programs for poor people that were initiated during
President Johnson's War on Poverty in the late 1960s (Mead, 1992). Some
poor consumers may exchange food stamps for consumables; single
mothers may obtain WIC foods for their children under age 5; AFDC can
be used to obtain housing, transportation, clothing, and other necessities
of life; housing subsidies can be exchanged for shelter; and Medicaid helps
pay for health care. It has been argued that this method of balancing the
exchange between poor consumers and marketers may lead to disincen-
tives for poor people to find other means of obtaining objects to exchange,
such as working to earn money (Mead, 1992; Murphy, 1994). It also has
been demonstrated that welfare benefits the poor. One example is that

nutritional needs of eligible nonrecipients of food stamps are not as well met as are those of recipients (Bishop et al., 1992).

A second approach is for government regulators or social service agencies to *increase the exchange power of poor consumers*. One way to increase the exchange power of poor consumers is to allow and encourage the poor to take more responsibility for how, when, and what they exchange. For example, some states are experimenting with "cashing out" food stamp programs. They allow purchases by food stamps to be determined by the recipient ("Debate Stirs," 1994). Other experimental programs offer electronic entitlement transfers similar to a debit card to poor people who are eligible for food stamps. This program has the potential to reduce poor peoples' need for more costly currency exchanges. This approach also can increase the exchange power of poor consumers by requiring that they take greater responsibility for budgeting their resources. Another way for poor consumers to increase their power in exchanges with marketers is to take advantage of an approach long used by businesses, saving by buying in quantity (discussed in the last section).

A third approach is to *decrease the exchange power of the marketer.* The marketer's advantage in exchange situations can be controlled by implicit societal mores, explicit governmental regulation, or explicit societal pressure. For example, outright violations of the laws of exchange, such as not delivering goods that have been paid for, are clearly unacceptable to society and are illegal. Unethical practices in advertising and in marketing of goods and services are controlled by numerous regulations at the federal, state, and local levels. An example of social pressure to decrease the exchange power of marketers can be seen in R. J. Reynolds's removal from the market of Uptown cigarettes, a brand targeted to low-income African Americans, after vociferous complaints from the community (Ramirez, 1990).

A fourth approach is to *alter what marketers have to exchange*. As markets mature, competition for market share frequently demands that products and services offer added value to the consumer (Park, Jaworski, & MacInnis, 1986). As a result, products or services that initially offered just functional value subsequently are marketed in a range of varieties. These enhancements may diminish their *incremental* value to the consumer and often raise the cost of the product or service. Many product categories in the United States are in the mature stage, and it is often difficult to find models that offer the basic functional value. Marketers who offer functional no-frills products or services at a fair price would be welcomed by low-income consumers as well as by more affluent consumers. This is an underexplored marketing opportunity.

A fifth approach is for regulators to *reduce the risk perceived by marketers* when they enter into exchanges with poor consumers. This approach includes establishing enterprise zones to reduce taxes for businesses that locate in low-income neighborhoods or waive regulations such as zoning laws to encourage marketing exchanges with poor consumers. For example, baby food manufacturers vie for contracts with states to provide WIC brands to mothers of young infants and children. The reduced risk to the firms is that their sales are guaranteed for a specified time period. In addition, they gain profit, and they have an opportunity to create brand-loyal consumers (Gibson, 1993).

Another example of this approach is to allow small businesses to become more competitive with larger ones by taking advantage of large-firm practices such as buying in quantity and passing the lower cost to the consumers. For example, the Hartford, Connecticut, Grocers' Association, a group of grocers in poor neighborhoods, pools resources to buy wholesale food in bulk and charges lower prices to their consumers. Note that in this case a public or social service agency facilitated the process of allowing the small businesses to compete effectively in low-income neighborhoods (Consumers Union, 1993).

PUBLIC AND SOCIAL POLICY IMPLICATION: SMALL BUYING GROUPS AS AN EXAMPLE

One approach to more equitably balancing the exchange between poor consumers and for-profit marketers is to increase the power of poor consumers. A way to accomplish this is for poor consumers to buy in quantity. Poor consumers, with their limited funds, are usually unable to stockpile products, and indeed, there is evidence that they purchase smaller quantities than do more affluent consumers (Kalyanam & Putler, 1994). If poor consumers organized into small buying groups, they would be able to buy larger quantities, which are generally offered at a lower cost. They would also wield more power in a marketing exchange. As an entity that purchases large quantities on a regular basis, a small cooperative buying group is more profitable and offers less risk and lower transaction costs to the marketer. There are also advantages to the members of a small buying group: cost savings for each member of the group, enhanced bargaining power, social and emotional support, learning from each other, and practicing interpersonal and decision-making skills. Small buying groups can be formed by poor consumers on their own, or they can be facilitated by regulators or social service agencies. The benefits of these groups for society are that costs of goods and services to the poor should decrease. In addition, because this system demands that each individual take responsibility for the group's actions, it teaches responsible societal habits. Finally, because the group reinforces the responsibility practiced by its members by group pressure, risk of failure is reduced for the sponsors.

Small buying groups can be modeled on the "borrowing circles" introduced in Bangladesh by Dr. Mohammad Yunus, who founded the Grameen Bank (Kamaluddin, 1993; Montemayor, 1993). This bank funds groups of five women for business projects. Every member of the borrowing circle is responsible for repayment of the loan. If it is not repaid, none of the five can apply for another loan. The amount of the first loan is small, but if it is paid back, subsequent loans can be larger. This model has been adopted by organizations in several other nations, including the United States, such as the Good Faith Fund in Arkansas and the Full Circle Fund of the Women's Self-Employment Project in Chicago (Welles, 1994; Zehr, 1992).

One of the key features of this model in all countries is that it has been limited to women because women are considered more financially responsible. Indeed, it has been reported (Carrington, 1994; Montemayor, 1993) that the loan repayment rate is exceptionally high in the United States and other nations. One reason it may work well for women may be that women's ethical behavior differs from men's (Gilligan, 1977; Gilligan & Attanucci, 1988). Because women tend to have a more interpersonal and caring perspective than do men, they tend to focus more on moral and ethical conflicts in terms of their effects on other people. For this reason, women who take responsibility as members of a group are likely to be particularly sensitive to the effects of ethical actions on the other members of the group (Eagly & Wood, 1991).

Because households headed by women constitute a disproportionately large segment of poor households, the small buying group approach to increasing the exchange power of poor consumers should have a high potential for success. It also may be readily adopted by poor women: Group buying was self-initiated by borrowing circles in Chicago (Connie

Evans, Executive Director of the Women's Self-Employment Project, personal communication, June 13, 1994).

Small cooperative groups have been successful in financing small businesses outside the United States in Korea, Japan, China, and parts of Africa. Koreans brought the *kye,* or rotating credit association (Consumers Union, 1993), to the United States to finance small businesses. A *kye* of a small group of people pools funds and rotates the pool of money around the group until all have received it. One of the problems with this system is that if the pool is lost in a bad business venture by an early participant, later participants suffer. One safeguard has been for early borrowers to pay a higher rate of interest than later ones, so there is a trade-off between the cost of borrowing and the risk of capital loss. Because *kyes* are informal groups that are unregulated, insurance against loss is absent, and a number of civil cases have resulted from *kye* disputes (Consumers Union, 1993).

Part of the reason for the success of revolving credit associations in non-European and non-North American parts of the world may have to do with the value placed on interpersonal relationships in these cultures (Markus & Kitayama, 1991, 1994). Unlike Western "independent" cultures in which a key personal goal is to maintain oneself as a unique individual, "interdependent" cultures of the non-Western world prize maintaining relationships with other people (Markus & Kitayama, 1994). In these interdependent cultures, the ethical constraints on fair deals within a small group must be much greater than in many parts of Western cultures. Markus and Kitayama (1994) point out that collectives like those suggested above often are considered threatening in the mainstream U.S. culture because they are inconsistent with our driving force of individuality. They also point out that marginalized groups, which might include poor people, are more inclined to favor an interdependent rather than an independent relationship with collectives such as small cooperative groups (p. 575)—it is the more privileged members of society who can afford to consider themselves as autonomous and value individualism.

PRACTICAL APPROACHES TO SOLUTIONS

To balance the marketing exchange more in favor of the poor consumer, behavior of the poor consumer, marketers, regulators, social service providers, and the public must be changed. How can behavior be changed? Here are six approaches. First, one can change attitudes of the public, of marketers, of regulators, and of the poor through education. People often act consistently with their attitudes, so behavior can be changed by altering the current attitudes of each of the parties to the exchange in appropriate ways. A better understanding of the makeup of the poverty population and the causes of poverty may help marketers act in an enlightened self-interest.

Second, societal norms might be altered to be more positive, compassionate, and understanding of the poor. This would seem to be a long-term task with little probability of much success, given the history of attitudes to poverty in the United States discussed in Chapter 1. Once again, however, a better understanding of the needs of the poverty population and the barriers poor people face together with a recognition that the poor share many attributes of mainstream society should help nonpoor members of society hold more compassion for the poor.

Third, the perception of self-efficacy by poor consumers can be enhanced so they perceive themselves as more powerful and are able to act consistently with that perception. Feelings of increased control over exchanges in the marketplace encourage the acceptance of more responsibility. The earlier discussion of small buying groups could be a way to enhance positive feelings of self-efficacy.

Fourth, public policymakers can use regulation to enforce behavior that serves to better balance marketing exchanges with poor consumers. Businesses and societal programs that can influence programs of social service providers are both potential targets of such regulation.

Fifth, public policymakers can use a carrot rather than a stick by offering incentives to marketers, poor consumers, social service providers, or to society as a whole to alter behavior in marketing exchanges that involve poor consumers. For example, public policymakers can reward early innovators by offering the highest incentives and support for the first businesses that enter inner-city low-income neighborhoods and the first poor consumers to form buying groups.

Sixth, through self-regulation, marketers can change the marketplace themselves.

SUMMARY OF RECOMMENDATIONS FOR MARKETERS

In the preceding chapters, we recognized that there are numerous barriers to businesses in developing equitable exchanges with poor consumers. We also offer specific recommendations for marketers with regard to poor consumers. These include the following:

- *Marketers must know the segment of poor consumers.* Marketers must correct their misconceptions about who are poor consumers, how much they have to spend, and what their needs are. Poor consumers are not all inner-city African American urban dwellers. A sole reliance on reported income understates the market potential of poor consumers, so reliance on marketing reports based on reported income can be misleading. Both retailers and manufacturers must recognize that most poor people are only temporarily in need, so building a long-term customer relationship with them has a high potential to be profitable.
- *Marketers should consider the conditions under which poor consumers can be ethically treated as a unique market segment.* This is a reasonable strategy for products that do poor consumers no harm, but it is not appropriate for products that will harm them directly or harm society as a whole. Furthermore, marketers must recognize that the poor are a diverse group and subgroups among them have different needs that can be satisfied by consumer goods.
- *Businesses can offer products and services that better serve the needs of poor consumers.* For example, businesses can offer a line of basic no-frills products that cost less to produce and market. Similarly, if retailers do not want to face the risks of locating in poor neighborhoods, they can subsidize public transportation or provide private transportation to facilitate use of their stores by poor consumers. Banks can offer financial management services to poor consumers that reduce risks to both the banks and the consumers.
- *Businesses can profitably locate retail stores in poor neighborhoods.* This is an alternative to operating offshore facilities, an option used, for example, by several restaurant chains and discount retail outlets. It serves the needs of poor communities, builds long-term relationships with consumers who are currently (but not likely permanently) poor, and is a profitable growth opportunity.

RECOMMENDATIONS FOR OTHER INSTITUTIONS

In prioritizing solutions, we argue for solutions that rely on self-reliance by poor consumers to solve their own problems with limited help of social service providers and possibly the government. For example, outside parties may facilitate actions poor consumers can take to solve their own problems. If these do not work sufficiently, then efforts by social service providers and the government should be mobilized. The protection, however, should be specific to areas of "market abuse."

Consider just two of the ways of changing behaviors mentioned above, regulation by public policymakers and changing attitudes (education). The people whose behavior is to be changed include the relevant parties

TABLE 9.2 Examples of Uses of Education and Regulation to Change Behavior
to Better Balance Marketing Exchanges With Poor Consumers

Change Attitudes of	By Education	By Regulation

Poor consumers	Self-efficacy
	Methods of coping with
	   marketing communications
	Ways to get more value for
	   money
	Financial management
		Checks on violation of welfare
		   fraud

Marketers	Correct stereotypes about
	   poor
	Awareness of profitability
	   of marketing to poor
	Awareness of needs of
	   segments of poor
	   consumers
	Shortcomings of annual data
		Ethical issues
		Reduce barriers to entry to poor
		   markets
		Control communication about
		   sin products
		Price discrimination
		Checks on violation of welfare
		   fraud

Public policymakers	Correct stereotypes of poor
	Shortcomings of annual data
	Price discrimination
	Difference between safety net
	   and bootstrap programs
		Determine best governmental
		   level at which to legislate or
		   implement regulation

Social service agencies	How to increase self-efficacy
	   of poor
		Determine how they can
		   implement legislation

Public	Correct stereotypes of poor Change attitudes to poverty	

to the exchange: marketers, public policymakers, social service providers, and the public. Table 9.2 presents examples of the goals for which each of these approaches to changing behavior might be used. For instance, welfare fraud is an example of a behavior that must be regulated, whereas correction of stereotypes of poor consumers can be changed by education.

CONCLUSION

Exchange in the current marketplace is tilted against poor consumers. This imbalance reinforces the place of the poor consumer as an outsider,

a stranger who is marginalized in our society. Not only does this margi-
nalization isolate the poor consumer from society, but it also encourages
that person to reject society's rules. It becomes increasingly difficult for
all parties to an exchange to redress the wrongs done to poor consumers
by businesses and the market structure if the poor consumer does not agree
with the same basic rules. The basis for marketing—marketing exchange—
breaks down, and a vicious cycle results. Therefore, it is necessary for the
poor consumer to be brought into the mainstream of consumer behavior
by both balancing exchange and by demanding ethical behavior by all of
the parties to marketing exchanges.

In this book, we discuss only one aspect of the lives of the poor—their
roles as consumers. We do not attempt to solve all of the problems of
poverty. Our recommendations and implications offer some specific and
some general ways in which to better the life of the poor consumer. Clearly,
many of the problems of the poor consumer must be solved by addressing
poverty as a broader issue. For instance, the key solution, as President
Lyndon Johnson indicated in the 1970s, undoubtedly lies with improving
education of the poor. We offer a multifaceted approach to bettering the
balance of marketing exchange that involves the poor consumer. In
particular, the focus should be to educate all parties to the exchange
regarding the needs and characteristics of the poor consumer and businesses, to encourage the establishment and maintenance of businesses in
poor areas, to develop and market products designed specifically to meet
the needs of poor consumers, and to enhance the ability of the poor
consumers to help themselves. Although none of these proposals are in
and of themselves magic bullets that will solve all the problems of the poor
consumer, jointly they can ease the predicament of poor consumers,
businesses that market to the poor, and society as a whole.

References

Ackerman, J. (1989, September 27). Bus riders fear route changes may disrupt lives. *Boston Globe*, p. 29.

Adler, N., Boyce, T., Chesney, M., Cohen, S., Folkman, S., Kahn, R., & Syme, L. (1994). Socioeconomic status and health: The challenge of the gradient. *American Psychologist, 49*(1), 15-24.

Allen, V. L. (1970). Personality correlates of poverty. In V. L. Allen (Ed.), *Psychological factors in poverty* (pp. 242-266). Chicago: Markham.

Alwitt, L. F. (1995). *Public perceptions of products consumed by the poor* (Working paper). Chicago: DePaul University.

Ambry, M. (1993). *The official guide to household spending* (2nd ed.). Ithaca, NY: New Strategist Publications and Consulting.

Anderson, J. R. (1983). *The architecture of cognition*. Cambridge, MA: Harvard University Press.

Andreasen, A. R. (1975). *The disadvantaged consumer.* New York: Free Press.

Andreasen, A. R. (1978). The ghetto marketing life cycle: A case of underachievement. *Journal of Marketing Research, 15,* 20-28.

Bagozzi, R. P. (1975). Marketing as exchange. *Journal of Marketing, 39,* 32-39.

Bagozzi, R. P. (1979). Toward a formal theory of marketing exchanges. In O. C. Ferrel, S. W. Brown, & C. W. Lamb, Jr. (Eds.), *Conceptual and theoretical developments in marketing* (pp. 431-447). Chicago: American Marketing Association.

Bane, M. J., & Ellwood, D. (1986). Slipping into and out of poverty: The dynamics of spells. *Journal of Human Resources, 21*(1), 1-23.

Barnard, K. (1992, May 5). The 90's: Decade of the discounter. *Discount Merchandiser, 32,* 76-78.

Bary, A. (1994, August 15). Used-car loans: Suddenly sexy. *Barron's, 74,* p. 18.

Bawa, K., & Shoemaker, R. W. (1987). The coupon-prone consumer: Some findings based on purchase behaviour across product classes. *Journal of Marketing, 51,* 99-110.

Belew, J. (1989). The unbanked. *Journal of Retail Banking, 6*(4), 55-56.

Bell, J., & Burlin, B. M. (1993). In urban areas: Many of the poor still pay more for food. *Journal of Public Policy and Marketing, 12*(2), 268-270.

Bellah, R. N., Madsen, R., Sullivan, W. M., Swidler, A., & Tipton, S. M. (1985). *Habits of the heart.* Berkeley: University of California Press.

Berkman, H. W., & Gilson, C. C. (1976). Social class and consumer behavior: A review for the 70's. *Journal of the Academy of Marketing Science, 4*(3), 644-657.

Bird, L. (1994, March 7). Baltimore measure clamps down on tobacco ads in private spaces. *Wall Street Journal,* p. B8.

Bishop, J. A., Formby, J. P., & Zeager, L. A. (1992). Nutrition and nonparticipation in the U.S. food stamp program. *Applied Economics, 24,* 945-949.

Blackburn, M. L. (1994). International comparisons of poverty. *American Economic Review, 84*(2), 371-374.

Blank, R. (1993). Why were the poverty rates so high in the 1980s. In D. Papdimitrious & E. Wolfe (Eds.), *Poverty and prosperity in the U.S. in the late twentieth century.* New York: St. Martin's.

Blank, R., & Blinder, A. (1986). Macroeconomics, income distribution, and poverty. In S. H. Danziger & D. Weinberger (Eds.), *Fighting poverty: What works and what doesn't* (pp. 182-208). Cambridge, MA: Harvard University Press.

Blattberg, R. C., & Neslin, S. A. (1990). *Sales promotion: Concepts, methods, and strategies.* Englewood Cliffs, NJ: Prentice Hall.

Blaylock, J. R. (1991). Variety, prices and food status in low-income households. *Applied Economics, 23,* 1019-1027.

Block, C. E. (1972). Pre-purchase search behavior of low income households. *Journal of Retailing, 48*(1), 3-15.

Bornstein, R. F. (1989). Exposure and affect: Overview and meta-analysis of research, 1968-1987. *Psychological Bulletin, 106,* 265-289.

Bould, S. (1977). Female-headed families: Personal fate control and the provider role. *Journal of Marriage and the Family, 39,* 339-349.

Bowers, J. S., & Crosby, K. (1980). Changes in the credit repayment performance of low income consumers: An exploratory study. *Journal of Consumer Affairs, 14*(1), 96-108.

Boyer, E. J., & Ford, A. (1992, May 8). Black-owned businesses pay a heavy price. *Los Angeles Times,* pp. A1, A5.

Bradford, C., & Cincotta, G. (1992). The legacy, the promise, and the unfinished agenda. In G. D. Squires (Ed.), *From redlining to reinvestment* (pp. 228-286). Philadelphia: Temple University Press.

Braus, P. (1991). One paycheck from the poorhouse. *American Demographics, 4*(11), 4, 13.

Bremner, B. (1990, October 8). Looking downscale without looking down. *Business Week* (Industrial edition), pp. 62-67.

Brostoff, S. (1993, February 15). Study cites homeowner insurer discrimination. *National Underwriter,* p. 6.

CACI Marketing Systems. (1994). *The sourcebook of ZIP code demographics* (8th ed.). Fairfax, VA: Author.

Caine, P. (1993, January). The dream that died. *Chicago Reporter,* pp. 3-7, 13.

Caplovitz, D. (1981). Making ends meet: How families cope with inflation and recession. *Annals of AAPSS, 446,* 88-98.

Capozza, D., & Van Order, R. (1978). A generalized model of spatial competition. *American Economic Review, 68*(5), 896-898.

Carrington, T. (1994, June 22). In developing world, international lenders are targeting women. *Wall Street Journal,* p. A1.

Caskey, J. P. (1991a, November/December). Check-cashing outlets in the U.S. financial system. *Economic Review,* pp. 53-67.

Caskey, J. P. (1991b). Pawnbroking in America: The economics of a forgotten credit market. *Journal of Money, Credit, and Banking, 23,* 85-99.

Cateora, P. R. (1990). *International marketing* (7th ed.). Homewood, IL: Irwin.

Cavusgil, T. S. (1982, October 15). Study finds three car aftermarket segments. *Marketing News, 16,* 7.

Chetwynd, J. (1994, September 23). Equity fund with $24 million formed to build malls in low-income areas. *Wall Street Journal,* p. B5a.

Chua, L. (1994, April 25). Opening up for business. *Los Angeles Times,* pp. D1, D2.

Clayton Act, 15 U.S.C. § 13 (1914).

Clee, M. A., & Wicklund, R. A. (1980). Consumer behavior and psychological reactance. *Journal of Consumer Research, 6,* 389-404.

Coe, B. D. (1971). Private versus national preference among lower and middle income consumers. *Journal of Retailing, 47*(3), 61-72.

Coe, R. (1978). Dependency and poverty in the short and long run. In G. J. Duncan & J. N. Morgan (Eds.), *Five thousand American families: Patterns of economic progress* (Vol. 6, pp. 273-296). Ann Arbor, MI: Institute for Social Research.

Consumers Union. (1993). *The thin red line: How the poor still pay more.* San Francisco: Consumers Union of the United States, West Coast Regional Office.

Cotterill, R. W., & Franklin, A. W. (1995, April). *The urban grocery store gap* (Food Marketing Policy Issue Paper No. 8). Storrs, CT: Food Marketing Policy Center, Department of Agricultural and Resource Economics, University of Connecticut.

Council of Economic Advisors. (1964). *Economic report of the president.* Washington, DC: Government Printing Office.

Council of Economic Advisors. (1984). *Economic report of the president.* Washington, DC: Government Printing Office.

Council of Economic Advisors. (1993). *Economic report of the president.* Washington, DC: Government Printing Office.

Customers bank on drugstores when paying utility bills. (1991, May 6). *Drug Topics,* p. 86.

Danziger, S., & Gottschalk, P. (1987). Earnings inequality, the spatial concentration of poverty, and the underclass. *American Economic Review, 77*(2), 211-215.

Danziger, S., van der Gaag, J., Taussig, M., & Smolensky, E. (1984). The direct measurement of welfare levels: How much does it take to make ends meet? *Review of Economics and Statistics, 66*(3), 500-505.

Davidson, J. (1995, May 12). Welfare mothers stress importance of building self-esteem if aid system is to be restructured. *Wall Street Journal,* p. A14.

Dawson, S., Stern, B., & Gillpatrick, T. (1990). An empirical update and extension of patronage behaviors across the social class hierarchy, social class. *Advances in Consumer Research, 7,* 833-838.

Debate stirs as states "cash out" food stamps. (1994, March 8). *Chicago Tribune*, p. 3.

Deighton, J., Romer, D., & McQueen, J. (1989). Using drama to persuade. *Journal of Consumer Research, 16,* 335-343.

DeParle, J. (1993, July 14). Census reports a sharp increase among never married mothers. *New York Times*, p. A9.

Diesenhouse, S. (1993, June 27). As suburbs slow, supermarkets return to the cities. *New York Times*, p. Fl.

Distilling the truth about alcohol ads. (1992). *Business and Society Review Symposium, 83,* 12-17.

Do Hispanic shoppers use coupons? (1988, May). *Chain Store Executive, 64,* 247-248.

Dominquez, L. V., & Page, A. L. (1981). Stratification in consumer behavior research: A re-examination. *Journal of the Academy of Marketing Science, 9*(3), 250-271.

Donley, T. (1994). The impact of consumption controls on the official poverty counts. *American Society of Business and Behavioral Sciences Perspectives Journal, 1*(1), 156-168.

Donthu, N., & Cherian, J. (1992). Hispanic coupon usage: The impact of strong and weak ethnic identification. *Psychology and Marketing, 9*(6), 501-510.

Duff, C. (1991, July 5). Priest who defaced billboards acquitted. *Wall Street Journal*, p. B2.

Duncan, G., Coe, R., & Hill, M. (1984). The dynamics of poverty. In G. J. Duncan (Ed.), *Years of poverty, years of plenty* (pp. 33-70). Ann Arbor, MI: Institute for Social Research.

Dun Analytical Services. (1994). *Industry norms and key business ratios.* Murray Hill, NJ:Dun and Bradstreet Information Services.

Dunn, W. (1986). In pursuit of the downscale. *American Demographics, 8,* 26-33.

Eagly, A. H., & Wood, W. (1991). Explaining sex differences in social behavior: A meta-analytic perspective. *Personality and Social Psychology Bulletin, 17,* 306-315.

Eckenrode, J. (1983). The mobilization of social support: Some individual constraints. *American Journal of Community Psychology, 5,* 509-528.

Exter, T. (1986). Looking for brand loyalty. *American Demographics, 8,* 32-33, 52-56.

Farley, R. (1988). After the starting line: Blacks and women in an uphill race. *Demography, 4,* 477-495.

Fehr, S. C. (1991, April 26). Old garage gives SE riders worst Metro buses in area. *Washington Post*, p. Cl.

Fields, R. (1995, June 11). Shopping trip becomes an ordeal. *Miami Sun-Sentinel*, p. 8a.

Fisher, C. (1990). Delivery systems foil couponing. *Advertising Age, 61,* 47.

Fisher, G. (1992). The development and history of the poverty thresholds. *Social Security Bulletin, 55*(4), 3-14.

Freedman, A. M. (1993, September 22). Peddling dreams: A market giant uses its sales prowess to profit on poverty. *Wall Street Journal*, pp. A1, A14.

French, N. D., & Lynn, R. A. (1971). Consumer income and response to price changes: A shopping simulation. *Journal of Retailing, 4,* 21-31.

Friestad, M., & Wright, P. (1994). The persuasion knowledge model: How people cope with persuasion attempts. *Journal of Consumer Research, 21*(1), 1-31.

Fuchs, V. (1967). Redefining poverty and redistributing income. *Public Interest, 8,* 88-95.

Fulgoni, G. M. (1988, June). Making advertising more effective. *Marketing Communications*, pp. 33-39, 76, 77.

Gallagher, R. (1989, July 7). Where America shops. *Chain Store Age Executive, 65,* 17-19.

Gelbtuch, H. C. (1990). The warehouse club industry. *Appraisal Journal, 58,* 153-159.

Gibbs, N. (1995, July 3). Working harder, getting nowhere. *Time*, pp. 16-20.

Gibson, R. (1993, March 29). U.S. aid plan for poor helps big food firms. *Wall Street Journal*, pp. B1, B6.

Gilligan, C. (1977). In a different voice: Women's conceptions of self and of morality. *Harvard Educational Review, 47,* 481-517.

Gilligan, C., & Attanucci, J. (1988). Two moral orientations. In C. Gilligan, J. V. Ward, J. M. Taylor, & B. Bardige (Eds.), *Mapping the moral domain* (pp. 73-86). Cambridge, MA: Harvard University Press.

Goedhart, T., Halberstadt, V., Kapteyn, A., & Van Praag, B. (1977). The poverty line: Concept and measurement. *Journal of Human Resources, 12,* 639-651.

Gordon, C. (1985, June 24). The trouble with garage sales. *Macleans, 98*(25), 9.

Gottschalk, P., & Danziger, S. (1984). Macroeconomic conditions, income transfers and the trend in poverty. In D. L. Bawden (Ed.), *The social contract revisited* (pp. 185-215). Washington, DC: Urban Institute Press.

Graham, R. (1981). The role of perception of time in consumer research. *Journal of Consumer Research, 7,* 335-342.

Granzin, K. L. (1981). An investigation of the market for generic product. *Journal of Retailing, 57*(4), 39-55.

Greenberg, D. I. (1980). Easy terms, hard times: Complaint handling in the ghetto. In L. Nader (Ed.), *No access to law* (pp. 379-415). New York: Academic Press.

Grzywinwki, R. (1991). The new old-fashioned banking. *Harvard Business Review, 69,* 87-98.

Gundlach, G. T., & Murphy, P. E. (1993). Ethical and legal foundations of relational marketing exchanges. *Journal of Marketing, 57,* 35-46.

Hacker, G. A., Collins, R., & Jacobson, M. (1987). *Marketing booze to blacks.* Washington, DC: Center for Science in the Public Interest.

Hagenaars, A., & Van Praag, B. (1985). A synthesis of poverty line definitions. *Review of Income and Wealth, 31*(2), 139-154.

Halverson, R. (1994, June 20). Bud's outlets attract downscale shoppers with big-ticket items at low payments. *Discount Store News,* pp. 78-80.

Hammel, F. (1991). A reason to cheer. *Supermarket Business, 46,* 43-50, 73.

Harris Poll. (1991). [Survey on file at University of North Carolina], IRSS Internet.

Harvey, F. B., III. (1987, Winter). The enterprise foundation approach to financing housing for poverty-level families. *Real Estate Finance Journal,* pp. 44-48.

Henderson, N. (1991a, September 4). Bus riders creating a storm. *Washington Post,* p. D1.

Henderson, N. (1991b, September 23). The ward that roared: Through bus battle, Anacostia finds its political voice. *Washington Post,* p. A1.

Hendon, D. W., Williams, E. L., & Huffman, D. E. (1988). Social class system revisited. *Journal of Business Research, 17,* 259-270.

Higgins, J. (1981). *States of welfare.* New York: St. Martin's.

Higgins, K. T. (1993). Getting the goons. *Credit Card Management, 5*(11), 20-26.

Hill, M. (1984). Some dynamic aspects of poverty. In G. J. Duncan (Ed.), *Years of poverty, years of plenty* (pp. 93-123). Ann Arbor, MI: Institute for Social Research.

Hill, R. P. (1994). Bill collectors and consumers: A troublesome exchange relationship. *Journal of Public Policy and Marketing, 13*(1), 20-35.

Hirst, E., & Talwar, R. (1981). Reducing energy consumption in low-income homes. *Evaluation Review, 5*(5), 671-685.

Hixon, R. M. (1991, March 18). Building business. *Mortgage Banking, 5,* 35-39.

Hoch, S. J., Kim, B. D., Montgomery, A. L., & Rossi, K. D. (1995). Determinants of store-level price elasticity. *Journal of Marketing Research, 32,* 92-136.

Hopfensberger, J. (1992, October 25). Growing up poor in Minnesota. *Minneapolis Star Tribune,* p. 1a.

Horton, J. (1967, April). Time and cool people. *Trans-Action,* pp. 4, 5-12.

Houston, F. S., Bassenheimer, J. B., & Maskulka, J. M. (1992). *Marketing exchange transactions and relationships.* Westport, CT: Quorum.

Howe, N., & Strauss, W. (1992). The new generation gap. *Atlantic Monthly, 270*(6), 67-89.

How viewers feel about TV. (1993). *American Demographics, 15,* 15, 18.

Hudson, M. (1993a, Summer). Should regulators check up on check cashers? *Business and Society Review,* pp. 47-50.

Hudson, M. (1993b, Fall). The poverty industry. *Southern Exposure,* pp. 16-27.

Hwang, S. L. (1994, November 2). Nutrament, debunked as a "fitness" drink, is reborn in the slums. *Wall Street Journal,* pp. A1, A6.

Ingram, B. (1993). A not-so-bountiful harvest this year? *Supermarket Business, 48,* 19-23.

Ingram, B. (1994). Hunger relief—less to bank on. *Supermarket Business, 49,* 191-196.

Internal Revenue Service. (1988). *Income tax compliance research* (Supporting appendixes to publication 7285). Washington, DC: U.S. Department of the Treasury.

Ippolito, P., & Mathios, A. D. (1991). Health claims in food marketing: Evidence on knowledge and behavior in the cereal market. *Journal of Public Policy and Marketing, 10*(1), 15-32.

Janofsky, M. (1995, April 5). Kool-Aid, not soda: Living on food stamps. *New York Times,* pp. A1, A10.

Jencks, C. (1994). *The homeless.* Cambridge, MA: Harvard University Press.

Joyal, V. (1992). The low-income household. *Executive, 32,* 37-43.

Kahneman, D., & Tversky, A. (1979). Prospect theory: An analysis of decisions under risk. *Econometrica, 47,* 263-291.

Kalyanam, K., & Putler, D. S. (1994). *A consistent framework for incorporating demographic variables in brand choice models* (Working paper). Chicago: DePaul University.

Kamaluddin, S. (1993). Lender with a mission. *Far Eastern Economic Review, 156,* 38-40.

Katcher, P. (1988). Under the hood. *American Demographics, 10,* 38-41.

Klein, H., & Pittman, D. J. (1990). Perceived consequences associated with the use of beer, wine, distilled spirits, and wine coolers. *International Journal of the Addictions, 25*(5), 471-493.

Koehn, D. (1992). Toward an ethic of exchange. *Business Ethics Quarterly, 2,* 341-355.

Kretzmann, M. J. (1992). Bad blood: The moral stigmatization of paid plasma donors. *Journal of Contemporary Ethnography, 4,* 416-441.

Kurian, G. T. (1991). *The new book of world rankings* (3rd ed.). New York: Facts on File.

Laczniak, G. R., & Murphy, P. E. (1993). *Ethical marketing decisions.* Boston: Allyn & Bacon.

Leading National Advertisers, Inc. (1991). *Class/brand $.* New York: Author.

Lee, W. N., & Callcott, M. F. (1994). Billboard advertising: A comparison of vice products across ethnic groups. *Journal of Business Research, 30,* 85-94.

LeRoux, M. (1987, February 9). Coupons make sense as tickets to product sales. *Advertising Age, 58*(6), S16.

Levedahl, W. J. (1988). Coupon redeemers: Are they better shoppers? *Journal of Consumer Affairs, 22*(2), 264-283.

Levine, D. (1988). *Poverty and society: The growth of the American welfare state in international comparison.* New Brunswick, NJ: Rutgers University Press.

Levy, F. (1977). *How big is the American underclass?* (Working paper 0090-1). Washington, DC: Urban Institute.

Lewin, T. (1994, October 25). Dehydrated-food plant in Texas is dedicated to effort to feed the hungry. *New York Times,* p. A14.

Lewis, O. (1969). The culture of poverty. In D. P. Moynihan (Ed.), *On understanding poverty* (pp. 187-200). New York: Basic Books.

Lewis, W. F. (1987). Telling America's story: Narrative form and the Reagan presidency. *Quarterly Journal of Speech, 73,* 280-302.

Longworth, R. C., & Stein, S. (1995, July 3). Middle class finds odd jobs may be only way to stay afloat. *Chicago Tribune,* Sec. 1, pp. 1, 6.

Lunt, P. (1992). How seven banks serve low income markets. *ABA Banking Journal, 84,* 57-66.

Luria, A. R. (1976). *Cognitive development.* Cambridge, MA: Harvard University Press.

Lutz, R. J., Mackenzie, S. B., & Belch, G. E. (1983). Attitude toward the ad as a mediator of advertising effectiveness: Determinants and consequences. In R. P. Bagozzi & A. M. Tybout (Eds.), *Advances in consumer research* (Vol. 10, pp. 532-539). Ann Arbor: Association for Consumer Research.

Mahoney, J. (1995, June). *The philosophical and moral underpinnings of ethics.* AMA Faculty Consortium on Ethics and Social Responsibility, Hofstra University, Hempstead, NY.

Major, M. J. (1994, February). Check cashing services offer new profits. *Bank Marketing,* pp. 55-59.

Malt liquors gain popularity, notoriety. (1992, March 31). *Beverage World, 111,* 8.

Markus, H. R., & Kitayama, S. (1991). Culture and self: Implications for cognition, emotion, and motivation. *Psychological Review, 98*(2), 224-253.

Markus, H. R., & Kitayama, S. (1994). A collective fear of the collective: Implications for selves and theories of selves. *Personality and Social Psychology Bulletin, 20*(5), 568-579.

Martineau, P. (1958). Social classes and spending behavior. *Journal of Marketing, 22,* 121-130.

Maslow, A. H. (1970). *Motivation and personality* (2nd ed.). New York: Harper & Row.

Maxwell, B., & Jacobson, M. (1989). *Marketing disease to Hispanics.* Washington, DC: Center for Science in the Public Interest.

McCarthy, M. J. (1994, November 8). Hunger among elderly surges: Meal programs just can't keep up. *Wall Street Journal,* pp. A1, A4.

McCracken, G. (1981). Culture and consumption: A theoretical account of the structure and movement of the cultural meaning of consumer goods. *Journal of Consumer Research, 8,* 71-84.

McCrohan, K. (1995, June). *Consumers in informal markets.* AMA Faculty Consortium on Ethics and Social Responsibility, Hofstra University, Hempstead, NY.

McCrohan, K., & Smith, J. D. (1987). Consumer participation in the informal economy. *Journal of the Academy of Marketing Science, 15,* 62-68.

McCrohan, K., Smith, J. D., & Adams, T. K. (1991). Consumer purchases in informal markets: Estimates for the 1980s, prospects for the 1990s. *Journal of Retailing, 67*(1), 22-50.

McCrohan, K. F., & Sugrue, T. F. (1995). *Socioeconomic profiles of consumers in informal markets* (Working paper). Fairfax, VA: George Mason University.

McEnally, M. R., & Hawes, J. M. (1984). The market for generic brand grocery products: A review and extension. *Journal of Marketing, 48,* 75-83.

Mead, L. M. (1992). *The new politics of poverty.* New York: Basic Books.

Mediamark Research, Inc. (1993). *MRI/Mediamark Research, Inc.* New York: Author.

Metro Chicago Information Center. (1994). *Community financial needs in the Chicago area.* Chicago, IL: Author.

Meyers, A. R., Hingson, R., Mucatel, M., Heeren, T., & Goldman, E. (1985). The social epidemiology of alcohol use by urban older adults. *International Journal of Aging and Development, 21*(1), 49-59.

Mikesell, J. L. (1994). State lottery sales and economic activity. *National Tax Journal, 67,* 165-171.

Miller, C. (1994, January 17). Rediscovering the inner city. *Marketing News, 28*(2), 1.

Miller, G. A., Galanter, E., & Pribram, K. H. (1960). *Plans and the structure of behavior.* New York: Holt.

Mitchell, A. A. (1983). Cognitive processes initiated by exposure to advertising. In R. Harris (Ed.), *Information processing research in advertising* (pp. 13-42). Hillsdale, NJ: Lawrence Erlbaum.

Mitchell, A. A., & Olson, J. C. (1981). Are product attribute beliefs the only mediator of advertising effects on brand attitude? *Journal of Marketing Research, 18,* 318-332.

Montemayor, B. T. (1993). Banking on the poor. *Far Eastern Economic Review, 156,* 29.

Murphy, D. J. (1994, July 18). The jaws of the welfare trap. *Investor's Business Daily, 69,* 1-2.

Murphy, P. E. (1978). The effect of social class on brand and price consciousness for supermarket products. *Journal of Retailing, 54*(2), 33-42.

National Research Council. (1995). *Measuring poverty: A new approach.* Washington, DC: National Academy Press.

Neidell, L. A., Boone, L. E., & Cagley, J. W. (1985). Consumer responses to generic products. *Journal of Academy of Marketing Science, 12*(4), 161-176.

Newton, J. M. (1977). Economic rationality of the poor. *Human Organization, 36*(1), 50-61.

New York City Department of Consumer Affairs. (1991). *The poor pay more . . . for less.* New York: Author.

Nichols-Casebolt, A. M. (1988). Black families headed by single mothers: Growing numbers and increasing poverty. *Social Work, 33,* 306-313.

Northrop, E. M. (1991). Public assistance and antipoverty programs or why haven't means-tested programs been more successful at reducing poverty? *Journal of Economic Issues, 25,* 1017-1027.

O'Curry, S. (1995). *Income source effects* (Working paper). Chicago: DePaul University.

Orshansky, M. (1963). Children of the poor. *Social Security Bulletin, 26*(7), 3-13.

Orshansky, M. (1965). Counting the poor: Another look at the poverty profile. *Social Security Bulletin, 28*(7), 3-13.

Orshansky, M. (1968, June). Demography and ecology of poverty. In *Proceedings of a Conference on Research on Poverty* (p. 28). Washington, DC: Bureau of Social Science Research, Inc.

Orshansky, M. (1969, February). How poverty is measured. *Monthly Labor Review,* pp. 37-41.

Ortmeyer, G. K. (1993). Ethical issues in pricing. In N. C. Smith & J. A. Quelch (Eds.), *Ethics in marketing* (pp. 389-404). Homewood, IL: Irwin.

Park, C. W., Jaworski, B. J., & MacInnis, D. J. (1986). Strategic brand concept-image management. *Journal of Marketing, 50,* 135-145.

Polakow, V. (1993). *Lives on the edge.* Chicago: University of Chicago Press.

Pollay, R. W. (1986). The distorted mirror: Reflections on the unintended consequences of advertising. *Journal of Marketing, 50,* 18-36.

Porter, M. E. (1995). The competitive advantage of the inner city. *Harvard Business Review, 73,* 55-71.

Products no longer determine the selection of retail outlets. (1991, April 1). *Marketing News, 25*(7), 9.

Pulley, B. (1995, April 28). Borough board approves East Harlem supermarket. *New York Times,* p. A16.

Raab, S. (1993, December 26). Agents follow food stamps ad fences. *New York Times,* Sec. 1, p. 31.

Rabelais, F. (1963). *Works.* In J. Bartlett (Ed.), *The shorter Bartletts' familiar quotations* (p. 307). New York: Pocket Books.

Rainwater, L. (1974). *What money buys: Inequality and social meanings of income.* New York: Basic Books.

Ramirez, A. (1990, January 12). A cigarette campaign under fire. *New York Times,* p. D1.

Rank, M. R. (1994). *Living on the edge: The realities of welfare in America.* New York: Columbia University Press.

Rawls, J. (1971). *A theory of justice.* Cambridge, MA: Harvard University Press.

Razzouk, N., & Gourley, D. (1982). Swap meets: A profile of shoppers. *Arizona Business, 29,* 8-12.

Reardon, P. T., & Thomas, J. (1995, May 17). Plan to cut welfare sounds alarm. *Chicago Tribune,* Sec. 2, pp. 1, 5.

Rector, R. (1992, September 3). America's poverty myth. *Wall Street Journal,* p. 10.

Renwick, T., & Bergmann, B. (1993). A budget-based definition of poverty: With an application to single parent families. *Journal of Human Resources, 28*(1), 1-24.

Roberts, S. D. (1991). Effects of sudden income loss on consumption and related aspects of life: A study of unemployed steel workers. *Research in Consumer Behavior, 5,* 181-214.

Rohe, W. M., & Stegman, M. A. (1992). Public housing home-ownership: Will it work and for whom? *Journal of the American Planning Association, 58,* 144-157.

Romano, J. (1992, October 25). Safety net for the hungry is collapsing. *New York Times,* Sec. 13, pp. 1, 11.

Rotter, J. B. (1966). Generalized expectancies for internal versus external control of reinforcement. *Psychological Monographs, 80*(1, Whole No. 609).

Ruggles, P. (1990). *Drawing the line: Alternative poverty measures and their implications for public policy.* Washington, DC: Urban Institute Press.

Ruggles, P., & Williams, R. (1989). Longitudinal measures of poverty: Accounting for income and assets over time. *Review of Income and Wealth, 35*(3), 225-243.

Russell, J. T., & Lane, W. R. (1992). *Kleppner's advertising procedure* (12th ed.). Englewood Cliffs, NJ: Prentice Hall.

Ryan, N. (1992, November 29). Discounting shop-around notion. *Chicago Tribune,* Sec. 7, pp. 1, 5.

Salling, M., & Harvey, M. E. (1981). Poverty, personality, and sensitivity to residential stressors. *Environment and Behavior, 2,* 131-163.

Sandmo, A. (1991). Economists and the welfare state. *European Economic Review, 35,* 213-239.

Sawyer, A. G., & Howard, D. J. (1991). Effects of omitting conclusions in advertisements to involved and uninvolved audiences. *Journal of Marketing Research, 28,* 467-474.

Schaninger, C. M., & Sciglimpaglia, D. (1981). The influence of cognitive personality traits and demographics on consumer information acquisition. *Journal of Consumer Research, 8*(2), 208-216.

Schank, R. C. (1990). *Tell me a story.* New York: Scribner.

Schiffman, J. R. (1990, January 22). After uptown, are some niches out? *Wall Street Journal,* pp. B1, B5.

Schiller, B. (1995). *Economics of poverty and discrimination.* Englewood Cliffs, NJ: Prentice Hall.

Schreiber, E. S., & Boyd, D. A. (1980). How the elderly perceive television commercials. *Journal of Communication, 30,* 61-70.

Schwabel, F. (1992, July 2). Urban consumers pay more and get less, and gap may widen. *Wall Street Journal,* pp. A1, A3.

Schwartz, J. (1987). Hispanic opportunities. *American Demographics, 9,* 56-59.

Selinger, I. C. (1993, May 10). The big lottery gamble. *Advertising Age, 64*(20), 22-28.

Shops in inner cities: A sip of something good. (1992, October 10). *The Economist,* pp. 30-31.

Simmons Market Research Bureau, Inc. (1991). *The 1990 Simmons study of media and markets.* New York: Author.

Simmons Market Research Bureau, Inc. (1992). *The 1991 Simmons study of media and markets.* New York: Author.

Simon, R., Riccardi, N., & Katz, J. (1994, July 30). Union angrily breaks off contract talks with MTA. *Los Angeles Times,* p. A1.

Sims, C. (1992, October 29). Under siege: Liquor's inner city pipeline. *New York Times,* pp. 1, 6.

Smeeding, T. M. (1977). The anti-poverty effectiveness of in-kind transfers. *Journal of Human Resources, 12*(3), 360-378.

Smeeding, T. M. (1991). Cross-national comparisons of inequality and poverty position. In L. Osberg (Ed.), *Economic inequality and poverty: International perspectives* (pp. 39-59). Armonk, NY: M. E. Sharpe.

Smith, C. J., & Hanham, R. Q. (1985). Regional change and problem drinking in the United States, 1970-1978. *Regional Studies, 19,* 149-162.

Smith, N. C., & Quelch, J. A. (1993). *Ethics in marketing.* Homewood, IL: Irwin.

Stangenes, S. (1993a, May 26). FHA lending uneven by race, study says. *Chicago Tribune,* Business section, pp. 1, 2.

Stangenes, S. (1993b, May 20). Study: Disparity in bank use by whites, minorities. *Chicago Tribune,* Business section, pp. 1, 2.

Statistical abstract of the United States. (Various years). Washington, DC: U.S. Bureau of the Census.

Stern, B. B. (1988a). How does an ad mean: Language in services advertising. *Journal of Advertising, 17*(2), 3-14.

Stern, B. B. (1988b). Medieval allegory: Roots of advertising strategy for the mass market. *Journal of Marketing, 52,* 84-94.

Stern, B. B. (1991). Who talks advertising? Literary theory and narrative "point of view." *Journal of Advertising, 20*(3), 9-22.

Stern, W. (1993, November 8). Of mules and men. *Forbes, 152*(11), 212.

Szymanski, D. M., & Busch, P. S. (1987). Identifying the generics prone consumer: A meta-analysis. *Journal of Marketing Research, 24*(4), 425-431.

Taub, S. (1983, March 31). Can Kmart come back again? *Financial World,* pp. 50-52.

Taylor, C. R., & Taylor, J. C. (1994). Regulatory issues in outdoor advertising: A content analysis of billboards. *Journal of Public Policy and Marketing, 13*(1), 97-107.

TEFAP and FEMA—what do they mean? (1994, Fall). *Chicago Anti-Hunger Federation News,* pp. 4, 5.

Teinowitz, I. (1992, May 25). Malt liquor shows muscle despite weak ad support. *Advertising Age, 63,* 12.

Thalheimer, R., & Ali, M. M. (1992). Demand for parimutuel horse race wagering with special reference to telephone betting. *Applied Economics, 24,* 137-142.

The emerging entrepreneur. (1990, January). *Inc.,* pp. 59-60.

The wholesale club industry. (1988). *Discount Merchandiser, 28,* 38-39.

They will gladly take a check. (1992, December 1). *New York Times,* pp. D1, D22.

30 million hungry in U.S., report says. (1992, September 10). *Washington Post,* p. A8.

Thomas, J. (1995, June 28). Riders claim Greyhound not the ticket for service. *Chicago Tribune,* Business section, pp. 1, 3.

Thomas, P. (1992, November 30). Persistent gap: Blacks can face a host of trying conditions in getting mortgages. *Wall Street Journal,* pp. A1, A4-A5.

Tocqueville, A. de. (1945). *Democracy in America*. New York: Random House. (Original work published 1839-1840)

Transportation's toll. (1993). *American Demographics, 15*, 12.

Traub, J. (1995, May 29). The political supermarket. *New Yorker*, pp. 41-44.

U.S. Bureau of the Census. (1990). *Census of retail trade, 1987: Zip code files on CD-ROM* [Machine-readable data files]. Washington, DC: Author.

U.S. Bureau of the Census. (1993a). Measuring the effect of benefits and taxes on income and poverty: 1992. *Current Population Reports* (Series P60-186RD). Washington, DC: Government Printing Office.

U.S. Bureau of the Census. (1993b). Poverty in the United States: 1992. *Current Population Reports* (Series P60-185). Washington, DC: Government Printing Office.

U.S. Department of Health Education and Welfare. (1976, April). *The measure of poverty: A report to Congress as mandated by the Education Amendments of 1974*. Washington, DC: Government Printing Office.

U.S. Department of Labor, Survey of Labor Statistics. (1992). *Consumer expenditure survey, 1989: Interview survey computer file*. Ann Arbor, MI: Inter-University Consortium for Political and Social Research Distributor.

U.S. House of Representatives, Committee on Ways and Means. (1991). *Overview of entitlement programs: 1991 green book*. Washington, DC: Government Printing Office.

Walden, M. (1991). Testing implications of spatial economics models: Some evidence from food retailing. *Journal of Consumer Affairs, 24*(1), 24-43.

Watts, H. (1967). The iso-prop index: An approach to the determination of differential poverty income thresholds. *Journal of Human Resources, 2*(1), 3-18.

Weiss, R. S. (1984). The impact of marital dissolution on income and consumption in single-parent households. *Journal of Marriage and the Family, 46*, 115-127.

Welles, E. O. (1994, May 1). It's not the same America. *Inc.*, pp. 82-98.

Wells, W. D. (1989). Lectures and dramas. In A. Tybout & P. Cafferata (Eds.), *Cognitive and affective responses to advertising* (pp. 13-20). Lexington, MA: Lexington Books.

Western Union offers long-distance cards targeted at the poor. (1993, May 11). *Wall Street Journal*, p. A9.

Whalen, B. F. (1981, March 19). Study measures impact of inflation on blacks' products, brand choices. *Marketing News, 14*, 1, 4.

Whalen, B. F. (1983, May 13). Illiteracy: The marketing research implications. *Marketing News, 16*, 1, 18.

Wilhelm, M. S., & Ridley, C. A. (1988). Unemployment induced adaptations: Relationships among economic responses and individual and marital well-being. *Journal of Consumer Behavior, 9*, 5-20.

Wilson, W. J. (1987). *The truly disadvantaged: The inner city, the underclass, and public policy*. Chicago: University of Chicago Press.

Woolley, S. (1993a, January 25). Neither fish nor fowl—but some call it foul. *Business Week*, pp. 75, 78.

Woolley, S. (1993b, April 5). Western Union banks on the "unbanked." *Business Week*, pp. 71-72.

Yavas, U., & Riecken, G. (1981). Heavy, medium, light shoppers and nonshoppers of a used merchandise outlet. *Journal of Business Research, 9*, 243-253.

Zajonc, R. (1968). The attitudinal effects of mere exposure. *Journal of Personality and Social Psychology Monograph, 1*(2), Part 2.

Zamichow, N. (1994, May 30). Alice in transit land. *Los Angeles Times*, p. B1.

Zehr, M. A. (1992). Imported from Bangladesh. *Foundation News, 33*, 28-32.

Zeithaml, V. A. (1985). The new demographics and market fragmentation. *Journal of Marketing, 49,* 64-75.

Zimmerman, S., & Fields, R. (1995, June 11). Food store survey finds poor pay more. *Miami Sun-Sentinel* (Broward Metro Edition), pp. 1A, 8A.

Zinn, L. (1992, December 14). Move over boomers. *Business Week,* pp. 74-82.

Index

About the Authors

Linda F. Alwitt received her Ph.D. from the University of Massachusetts at Amherst. She is an Associate Professor in the Department of Marketing at DePaul University. Prior to joining DePaul University, she was an Associate Research Director at Leo Burnett Company, an advertising agency. She is a past president of the Society for Consumer Psychology (Division 23 of the American Psychological Association). She is the coeditor of *Psychological Processes and Advertising Effects* and a member of the editorial boards of the *Journal of Consumer Psychology* and the *Journal of Advertising Research*. She has published articles on consumer behavior, consumer reactions to for-profit and not-for-profit advertising, and perceptions of the worthiness of fund-raising organizations in several journals, including the *Journal of Advertising Research, American Behavioral Scientist,* and the *Journal of Marketing*.

Thomas D. Donley received his Ph.D. in Economics in 1993 from the University of Wisconsin—Madison, where he was employed as a Research Assistant for the Institute for Research on Poverty. He is an Assistant Professor of Economics at DePaul University. His research focuses on issues in income distribution and the poverty population with particular focus on the consumption patterns of the poor.